W9-BUE-662

# Starting Small Groups—
# and Keeping Them Going

**Why start small groups**

**How to organize small groups**

**How to train leaders**

Augsburg Fortress, Minneapolis

## About the Writers

The writers of *Starting Small Groups—and Keeping Them Going* have experience in a variety of small group settings. David Mayer, who has begun and facilitated small groups in a number of churches, serves as an assistant to the bishop of the Northwestern Pennsylvania Synod of the Evangelical Lutheran Church in America. He wrote Part 1, "Understanding Small Groups."

Nancy Vogel, writer of Part 2, "Organizing Small Groups in Your Church," serves as an associate in ministry and small group developer at Lutheran Ministry in Christ, Coral Springs, Florida.

The author of several books and formerly the associate pastor for small groups at Red Hill Lutheran Church in Tustin, California, George S. Johnson is the senior pastor of Cambridge Lutheran Church in Cambridge, Minnesota. He wrote Part 3, "Training Small Group Facilitators."

Harold Webb Eppley and Rochelle Yolanda Melander, editors and compilers of this resource, are husband and wife, ordained Evangelical Lutheran Church in America pastors, and a freelance writing team. They reside in Wauwatosa, Wisconsin.

## Credits

Developed in cooperation with the Division for Congregational Ministries.

George S. Johnson, David Mayer, and Nancy Vogel, writers

Harold Webb Eppley and Rochelle Yolanda Melander, compilers and editors

Andrea Lee Schieber and William Congdon, editors

The Wells Group and David Meyer, cover design

RKB Studios Inc., interior design

Scripture quotations unless otherwise noted are from the New Revised Standard Version of the Bible, copyright 1989 Division of Christian Education of the National Council of the Churches of Christ in the United States of America. Used by permission. Scripture quotations marked NIV are from The Holy Bible, New International Version®. Copyright © 1973, 1978, 1984 International Bible Society. Used by permission of Zondervan Publishing House. All rights reserved. The "NIV" and "New International Version" trademarks are registered in the United States Patent and Trademark Office by International Bible Society. Use of either trademark requires the permission of International Bible Society.

Copyright © 1995 Augsburg Fortress.

All rights reserved.

ISBN 0-8066-0125-6

Printed on 50% recycled paper (10% postconsumer fibers)

Manufactured in U.S.A.

1 2 3 4 5 6 7 8 9 0 1 2 3 4 5 6 7 8 9

# Contents

89771

# Introduction

If you have picked up this book, perhaps you know that small groups have nurtured the faith of millions of Christians throughout the history of the church as well as in recent years. People who make up small groups minister to unchurched persons, incorporate new members into churches, and provide an experience of community and spiritual growth for Christians of all ages.

Since the 1970s, a number of small group resources have been available to churches. You may have enthusiastically made use of these materials, yet are looking for new approaches and perspectives. Or you may recognize the power and potential of small groups, but for any number of reasons hesitate to implement small groups in your own locale.

If you find yourself at one of these crossroads, consider the following about *Starting Small Groups— and Keeping Them Going*. This resource is designed to help church leaders who:

☞ Recognize the reality that people today search for a sense of community and a faith that addresses their deepest needs

☞ Look for material that grows out of a solid biblical foundation and Christian tradition

☞ Want to balance the personal spiritual growth that small faith communities nurture with involvement in the larger church and mission motivated service

☞ Have limited time and want effective, thorough, and proven approaches to implementing new programs or expanding existing ones

*Starting Small Groups—and Keeping Them Going* is an all-in-one resource that helps church leaders each step of the way, whether you already have small groups underway or are just now planning to get started. This manual comprises three parts: "Understanding Small Groups," "Organizing Small Groups in Your Church," and "Training Small Group Facilitators." You can use the manual in its entirety or choose the material that best suits your situation.

"Understanding Small Groups" explores the central role of small groups in the Scriptures and throughout the history of the Christian church, including their popularity today. Building on the principles of small groups found in these biblical and historical models, this section provides basic criteria for faithful contemporary small groups.

"Organizing Small Groups in Your Church" guides you through the steps necessary for developing and implementing an intentional ministry through small groups. This section provides approaches for churches of various sizes and resources. It addresses the need for both pastoral and lay leadership in implementing the effort.

Organizing the effort and training small group facilitators are key to keeping your small group effort going. "Training Small Group Facilitators" provides valuable information for the people responsible for training small group leaders or facilitators in your church. This section includes five training sessions, plus a session for the facilitators of support and recovery groups. Background information and follow-up ideas for ongoing training of facilitators and church leaders are also presented.

Finally, this manual contains an abundance of reproducible training exercises and resource materials for a church planning team and small group personnel.

*Starting Small Groups—and Keeping Them Going* serves as a signpost for Intersections Small Group Series, which is part of a new generation of small group materials. The series includes a variety of books for small group use. Intersections resources are based on a small group model that includes three basic types of groups:

☞ Discipleship groups—where people gather to grow in Christian faith and life

☞ Support and recovery groups—which focus on special interests, concerns, or needs

☞ Ministry groups—which have a task-oriented focus

The listing under "Resources," page 137, identifies additional resources that are part of the Intersections Small Group Series.

As you review this manual and use it to begin or expand your church's small group effort, keep in mind that the Holy Spirit transforms lives and that in community we are challenged to grow in Jesus Christ. As people gather to share life stories and experiences, God's Spirit can work to enlighten and direct us. Together we become what we could not become alone. It is God's plan that it be so.

# 1

# Understanding Small Groups

# Understanding Small Groups

## Today's context

"Why don't we have more Bible study and prayer groups in our church?" asked Helen. She wasn't the first to ask. Her question reflected a growing interest among church members in ministry through small groups. Helen was looking for a place where she could experience more intimate community and a deeper spirituality.

In America today, four out of every ten people belong to a small group of some kind, and the number keeps growing. Half of these small groups are religious in nature, and participants overwhelmingly speak about finding community and a deeper faith in these gatherings.

Robert Wuthnow, in his book *Sharing the Journey* (Macmillan, 1994), gives an analysis of this unfolding trend. He contends that the small group movement is a quiet revolution taking place in today's society that is altering the way we view God and relate to one another. He says that we are a society in transition where people search for a sense of community and for the sacred. The combination of these two has given impetus to the increasing interest in gathering people in small groups.

This phenomenon provides churches with an exciting opportunity for strengthening Christian community and for welcoming unchurched people. Yet, Helen's questions and comments are not the only ones expressed recently.

"What's this small group stuff about, anyway?" inquired Bob, a particularly traditional church member. "Are you going to make us all try some new program?" Bob did not like new activities in his church. He needed assurance that he wouldn't be forced to participate in small groups and, more important, that there is nothing new about small groups in the church.

Bob raised legitimate concerns. Church members and their leaders, even when they are open to change, don't like to be inundated with new programs every year. Responsible church leaders seek to test the faithfulness of new programs and emphases before they commit their time and resources to implementing them. Small groups can stand up to this scrutiny and have been tested by time. Small groups have served the needs of God's people since the days of Moses.

## Biblical practice

In the wilderness, the Israelites expected Moses to resolve all of their disputes (Exodus 18). Overwhelmed by the task, Moses followed the advice of Jethro, his wise father-in-law. He organized the Israelites into groups of ten. Moses presided over the difficult cases; all other issues were decided in the small groups.

Generations later, following the exile, the Jewish nation affirmed small groups in another way. The Law of Minyan states that the Torah may be read and worship conducted when there are ten adult males present.

Jesus reacted to this law, and to its apparent legalism and sexism, when he declared, "Where two or three are gathered in my name, I am there among them" (Matthew 18:20). Small groups, gathered in Jesus' name, became a gift of God, a means of grace. Christ creates this Christian community, regardless of the number, gender, race, or type of people that gather.

The gathering and sending of the first twelve disciples provides one of the best models for ministry through small groups. Jesus taught a small group of apprentice teachers. He showed them how to live together and he sent them out to heal and later to teach and baptize. Jesus' disciples participated in many of the activities that are central to contemporary small groups: prayer, community, teaching, evangelism, and sharing a meal.

In addition to teaching in the synagogue and in public places, Jesus frequently instructed his followers in quiet settings. The Gospels, especially Luke, tell many stories of Jesus and other followers, some of whom were women, gathering in homes. Homes not only served as the location for dramatic healings and the Last Supper, they also provided the settings for many parables and stories of the kingdom.

After Jesus' ascension and the birth of the church, small gatherings in homes emerged again (Acts 2:1-4). The Holy Spirit empowered an unlikely band of followers and they began to emulate their Lord. Acts 2:44-47 states, "All who believed were together and had all things in common; they would sell their possessions and goods and distribute the proceeds to all, as any had need. Day by day, as they spent much time together in the temple, they broke bread at home and ate their food with glad and generous hearts, praising God and having the goodwill of all the people. And day by day the Lord added to their number those who were being saved" (see also Acts 5:42).

Believers offered their homes as gathering places for the faithful. The house churches, small evangelical communities of up to forty people, emerged as the foundational structure of the apostolic church. Paul's letters and the book of Acts give detailed testimony to this fact. In Acts 20:20 he states, "I did not shrink from doing anything helpful, proclaiming the message to you and teaching you publicly and from house to house." Paul taught and wrote to the churches in the homes of many faithful women and men including Aquila and Priscilla (1 Corinthians 16:19); Philemon, Apphia, and Archippus (Philemon vv. 1-2); Chloe (1 Corinthians 1:11); and to many other unnamed churches (Romans 14–16; 1 Corinthians 1, 16; Colossians 4:15).

> The gathering and sending of the first twelve disciples provides one of the best models for ministry through small groups.

for women. The emergence of monastic and convent communities reflects the Christian community's desire for other opportunities to extend the fellowship of worship to everyday life. These communities of men and women took seriously Paul's words: "Do not be conformed to this world, but be transformed by the renewing of your minds, so that you may discern what is the will of God—what is good, acceptable and perfect" (Romans 12:2).

To each generation God gave the gift of community for the transformation and renewal of the church. Whenever the Christian community's vitality waned, new leaders and movements arose, seeking to renew the church. St. Francis founded the Franciscan Order. John Wesley initiated Methodist classes which sought to overcome institutional stagnation and the decline of the established churches. Dietrich Bonhoeffer formed small confessing church seminaries. Dorothy Day organized the Catholic Worker's Movement to break with a sterile conformity.

Today faith-centered small groups abound. Many Christians wonder if we are once again seeing God's gift of community through small groups offered to us as a means of transforming our individual and corporate lives. Others fear that we are merely witnessing another expression of twentieth-century religious faddism.

God gives us Christian community, *koinonia*. How we use or abuse that gift will ultimately tell the story of its transforming influence in our lives and its faithfulness to the gospel.

## A tradition of church renewal

The house church continued to be the primary setting for worship, teaching, and sending out until Constantine legalized Christianity in 313 A.D. When the practice of Christianity became legal, house churches gave way to congregations housed in their own buildings. Yet, throughout the centuries, small groups consistently reappeared in the church's life as vehicles for reformation and renewal.

Only five years after Constantine legalized Christianity, Pachomius and his sister Mary founded eleven monasteries in Egypt, nine for men and two

## Faithful small groups

With such a wide variety of small group programs and materials being offered, it is essential that we have some way of testing their faithfulness to the gospel and the apostolic tradition. The following four guidelines for measuring the quality of a church's small groups can provide that needed evaluation.

### Small groups listen to God

A faithful small group has vertical dimensions. The group gathers in the name of Jesus. The group centers its meeting on prayer and biblical reflection. The participants rely on God's Word and will. Without this component, small groups can tend to create their own godliness or to reshape God to their liking. Misusing this element refashions God into a deity whom we can manipulate or control. Faithful small groups are not only marked by their connectedness to God, but they are also spiritual schools where individual Christians learn to pray. For many Christians, prayer is either totally private or limited to corporate worship. Some Christians regard the ability and willingness to pray with others as a special gift possessed by the clergy and a few lay persons. Within the safe confines of a small group, Christians learn to pray aloud with others and share one another's concerns.

## Small groups are caring places

The group spends significant time sharing the joys and failures of individual lives. Groups respond with support, empathy, and love. Without this component, small groups either intellectualize the good news or function as purely task-oriented groups that take little notice of or time for the human need for community and compassion. Frequently, small groups become so compulsive about doing or learning something that they lose their identity as Christian communities. This lack of caring keeps many church classes and committees from ever becoming places of faithful transformation.

Many people in our culture prize individualism at the expense of community. Social networks in the family, neighborhood, and nation are in disarray. Small groups provide a setting where community can be experienced and built. For many participants, small groups serve as surrogate families that provide the loving relationships and responsibilities which make living in our society possible. However, special attention is required so that small groups do not also become isolated cells in the body of Christ.

## Small groups relate to the church

Small groups are not splinters or sects filled with special believers. Whatever the local church's polity may be, mechanisms for accountability in leadership, content, and group dynamics need to be in place and frequently evaluated by the church's leadership. Small groups that operate in isolation from the rest of the church may begin to consider it their ministry rather than part of the church's ministry.

Many pastors and lay leaders can recount horror stories of how the Wednesday morning prayer group or its equivalent began to degenerate into a gripe session that became the leaven for conflict and division in the church. Frequently the problem stems from the lack of oversight by the church and the lack of ongoing leadership training and accountability. Church leaders need to articulate clear understandings about the role of small groups within the church from the start and review them regularly.

Small groups do not replace Sunday worship. They grow out of the worshiping community for its renewal.

## Small groups welcome the stranger

Faithfulness to Jesus' Great Commission (Matthew 28:19-20) compels small groups to share the gospel with others. Outreach to the community and attention to evangelism are critical. Faithful small groups invite and welcome the stranger. When a small group neglects acts of hospitality, an exclusiveness enters into the life of the group which scares off newcomers and breeds the mistrust of others within the church. Faithful small groups are never secret meetings of the initiated but joyful gatherings of pilgrims inviting others to share the journey.

Once again, small groups serve as spiritual schools where Christians learn how to share the gospel more effectively. In small groups we can pray for those who are nonbelievers and for the opportunity to welcome them. An empty chair always waiting to be filled functions as a poignant reminder and as motivation for evangelism. The mutual encouragement of participants empowers the group to share the good news of Jesus Christ with neighbors and acquaintances.

## The Holy Spirit's work

Each of these criteria stresses a relationship: to God, to one another, to the church, and to the stranger. Forgetting any one of those relationships conforms Christians to the ways of this world and stifles the creative intentions of God through community. Without God at the center, the gift of community is lost. As Dietrich Bonhoeffer noted in *Life Together,* "It is easily forgotten that the fellowship of Christian brethren is a gift of grace, a gift of the Kingdom of God that any day may be taken from us..." (page 20).

People don't start or join small groups because the groups will be successful, because they are a great church growth strategy, or because they will meet the psychological needs of today's Christian. Small groups are not primarily a new program, another entry point, or a way to incorporate members. All or some of these may result from their development, but none of them is the reason for beginning such groups. People begin and join small Christian communities because it is faithful to do so. God has given us this gift and we are called to share it with one another.

Today the church is reclaiming its biblical and historical gift of Christian community. We may call it small group ministry, fellowship groups, or *koinonia*. We may try to fashion them and shape them to fit the days and worlds in which we live. And we will fail in our attempts if we do not call upon the strength of the Holy Spirit and affirm the great cloud of witnesses who have gone before us. Small groups are not our creation but the Holy Spirit's work among us. Christian community is a mighty act of God that elicits joy, awe, and humility and renews the church for its mission in the world.

**God has given us this gift and we are called to share it with one another.**

Sinclair Lewis, at the beginning of his novel *Dodsworth,* includes the claim, "It was 1903, the climax of all civilization" (page 1). That line sounds more foolish as each year passes. By our nature as human beings, we claim more for ourselves and our time than we deserve. Today's small group efforts build on a long history. Today we are not at the climax, but are only reclaiming a great and faithful inheritance that can once again transform and renew our churches and lives.

# 2

# Organizing Small Groups In Your Church

# Introduction

A focus on small groups as an intentional part of a church's ministry carries with it the expectation that these groups are Christian communities, where people grow in faith, share the good news of Jesus Christ, and serve God with joyful hearts. This is a relational model for ministry different from more task-oriented approaches common to many churches.

A small group emphasis also provides many choices for people to connect in a meaningful way to the larger faith community and further develop their spiritual gifts. A small group emphasis encompasses present members who are growing in faith and new members who are starting or continuing their faith journey in a new community. Another part of the population that responds to small groups is unchurched people, who for a variety of reasons have chosen not to participate in worship services or become active in a church.

Introducing an intentional, relational model of small groups into a church is proposing change. Change, even when perceived as good, can be met with challenges. Expect and celebrate those challenges,

• • • • • • • • • • • • • • •

**"Resistance is always greatest when change comes as a surprise."**

**(Dr. John Maxwell)**

Elmer L. Towns, *10 Of Today's Most Innovative Churches,* page 40.

• • • • • • • • • • • • • • • •

for no change should be implemented for the sake of change itself. Involving church members in a thoughtful process to understand why change is needed and how the change will be carried out will go a long way in building your small group effort.

Understanding the unique gifts, size, and local context of your church will help in planning. Introducing change in a slow, methodical manner assists all persons involved to adjust and accept a new emphasis. Customizing the approach to fit the needs of your church and the community in which it serves then becomes an evolutionary process, minimizing the negative effects of change.

"Organizing Small Groups in Your Church" offers practical suggestions to guide you in the process of developing and customizing a relational ministry through small groups. This section of the manual starts at ground level with building a foundation for small groups, then moves to studying your church, implementing small groups, ongoing development of your intentional small group effort, integrating new members, and final words of caution and encouragement.

# Building a Foundation

# Chapter 1

Small groups provide a place where people can be nurtured by God's saving grace and renewed for ministry in the world. Small groups provide a forum for healing and making disciples. They can function as a church's side door. We walk through the front door when we attend worship each week. Small groups provide an opportunity for involvement, study, discipleship, outreach, and support that is not always found in the larger Christian gathering. Small groups reach people in a different way and can serve as a building block of the church's ministry. Some people who are not reached through traditional worship services are attracted to the church's message through small groups.

What defines a small group? Roberta Hestenes, a leader in small group development, states that "a Christian small group is an intentional face-to-face gathering of three to twelve people on a regular time schedule with the common purpose of discovery and growing in the possibilities of the abundant life in Christ" ("Building Christian Community through Small Groups," page 27).

Essential components of small groups include biblical reflection, whether a longer Bible study or brief devotion; mutual support through intentional community building; group ministry beyond itself; and prayer.

## Types of small groups

Three basic types of small groups exist:

☞ Groups that focus on spiritual growth

☞ Groups that focus on nurture

☞ Groups that are task oriented

Traditional types of small groups within a congregation include committees (commissions or boards), single-task groups, Bible studies, issue studies, fellowship groups, and support and recovery groups.

For the purpose of this resource, these three basic types of groups will be called:

☞ Discipleship groups

☞ Support and recovery groups

☞ Ministry groups

See "Types of Small Groups" (Program Resource 1, page 16).

Discipleship groups focus on studying the Bible, an issue such as racism, or a faith development topic such as evangelism. Support and recovery groups gather around common human experiences such as parenting, communication, relationships, grief, and divorce. Ministry groups cover a wide spectrum of small groups. Their common characteristic is that they are task oriented, including such functions as coordination of Christian education, property maintenance, and worship planning, or single task activities such as collecting clothes for a clothes closet, organizing a world hunger walk, mowing lawns, acolyting, or making banners.

## Organizational approaches

Small groups exist in all churches, yet vary in whether the effort is intentional and how it is organized. Looking at different organizational approaches can help you understand the potential for developing or expanding an intentional small group emphasis in your church.

### Independent approach

This approach to organizing small groups is usually found in churches with 1 to 150 active members. Leaders coordinate the overall ministry of the church with small groups that address immediate needs. These groups are loosely coordinated, primarily task oriented, and managed by "familiarity"—people who know everyone else in the congregation.

### Accountable approach

This organizational approach is usually found in churches with 100 to 350 active members where there is need for more accountability. The church organizes around committees to distribute the responsibility for tasks and allow for a larger population where personal contact with everyone is not possible. Leaders often receive a basic orientation to the organization.

## Specialized approach

Some churches add small groups to their existing independent or accountable approaches to organizing their ministry. In this approach, small groups specialize in areas such as support (for example, grief or parenting) and discipleship (for example, Bible study or growth topic). Often a committee, volunteer coordinator, or a staff person develops and manages the effort. Leaders or facilitators are trained for the specific type of group and receive ongoing support. Curriculum or curriculum guidelines are used to address the specific concerns of each small group.

## Integrated approach

This approach considers all small groups in any size church part of an intentional small group network. All group meetings intentionally include key small group dynamics of prayer, biblical reflection, ministry task, and mutual support. Facilitators of all small groups receive training and ongoing support. Bible and other content guidelines are specific to each type of group. Church and staff support coordination and development.

The specialized and integrated approaches are examples of intentional small groups. Some components of intentional small groups may be present in the independent and accountable approaches also. For example, they might contain one of more of the following:

- Maximum size of twelve people
- Trained facilitators
- Accountable facilitators
- A balance of prayer, biblical reflection, mutual support, and ministry task
- People taking priority over agendas
- Regular meetings
- Curriculum or curriculum guidelines specific to the type of small group
- Coordination by a committee, volunteer, or staff

The benefits of small groups include:

- Provide a safe setting where confidentiality is expected and no one is judged
- Offer a supportive environment where a safety net of people care for people
- Encourage community through fellowship opportunities
- Help people discover individual spiritual gifts and highlight their uniqueness as children of God
- Develop active disciples as people live out their faith in daily life
- Provide opportunities for spiritual growth
- Find avenues for service to God
- Generate leaders for the church from within each small group
- Multiply into more small groups as new people participate

## Are small groups needed in your church?

To determine whether small groups are viable in your church, consider the following ten questions:

1. Are church members seeking to better understand how the Bible applies to their life situation?

2. Has the work of committees become a chore rather than a blessing?

3. Do members need personal care beyond what the staff can provide?

4. Do members need opportunities to identify, use, and further develop their spiritual gifts?

5. Do members and potential members need opportunities to connect with one another?

6. Do members seek opportunities outside of worship to hear and receive God's grace?

7. Is there a need to develop leaders in your church?

8. Has your membership failed to increase in numbers for several years due to members leaving or moving into inactivity?

9. Is your church searching for new ways to retain members and reach inactive members?

10. Does your church have a commitment to reaching people who are unchurched? Should your church have a commitment to reaching people who are unchurched?

If you've answered yes to even one of these questions, small groups can enhance your church's ministry. The next step is to involve others in the process of exploring the potential of small groups in your church.

# Initial developers

In smaller churches (under 200 members), the pastor or a lay member might introduce the small group concept and then often the pastor develops and coordinates small groups. In a larger church (more than 200), a pastor or a lay person may present the concept and turn over the development and administration to a group, a volunteer coordinator, or another staff person.

The pastor(s) and other recognized leaders must support an intentional small group emphasis as part of the church's vision for ministry. Generally, church members are more likely to get behind an effort if the pastor claims it as a priority. Therefore, involving the pastor in the initial development stage is critical. Involve respected lay leaders as initial developers, people who will promote the concept to others and take responsibility for further development of the effort.

Determine who the initial developers will be and involve them in creating a planning team.

## Planning team

A planning team reviews, evaluates, and recommends the appropriate approach to small groups for your church. The planning team members advocate the recommended structure and support lay leaders and existing ministry staff. Planning team members can take what they have learned about small group components back into the existing groups in which they participate and try them.

Consider the following factors in the formation of your planning team:

**Church size:** In a smaller church, the planning team may be the pastor and one or two key leaders. In a larger church, a planning team may be 10 to 12 people, including staff.

**Leadership attitude:** Key to each participant on this team is his or her willingness to consider all options for ministry that will build Christ's church, both numerically and spiritually.

**Leadership gift:** Persons on this team can bring diverse gifts to the team such as vision casting, organization, computer literacy, public speaking, and knowledge of the church's personality (historical background).

**Leadership structure:** The planning team might have representatives from specific interest groups such as education, stewardship, evangelism, and youth.

**Leadership visibility:** The planning team needs people who are visible and credible to the church.

## Future personnel needs

As your small group effort continues, personnel needs will be influenced by the following:

**Vision:** The purpose of the small group emphasis as it relates to the church's vision must constantly be put before church members. Highlighting the purpose serves to reaffirm the planning team's commitment through all successes and challenges. To keep growing, a church must keep going.

**Size of small group emphasis:** A healthy small group effort will grow and require staffing structures that grow. Examples include:

- ☛ A church might need to move from one pastor coordinating the effort to a pastor and a committee or board.

- ☛ A volunteer coordinator or committee might need to be replaced by a paid staff person dedicated to developing and coordinating small groups.

- ☛ A staff person assigned small groups might need to develop volunteer coordinators that assist in supporting and training small group facilitators.

- ☛ Multiple staff persons might coordinate small groups by their specific areas of ministry: for example, youth, young adults, or older adults.

- ☛ Multiple staff persons might organize around specific issues, such as director of support and recovery ministries, or minister of discipleship groups.

**Budget:** Finances usually dictate that a church start small and slowly, and develop leadership as the effort grows.

As the need for leadership grows, remember that structure serves the mission of the church and is limited only by the creativity, commitment, and resources that the church dedicates to its development.

The next chapter outlines the work of the planning team in studying your church to determine what approach to small groups will be most effective.

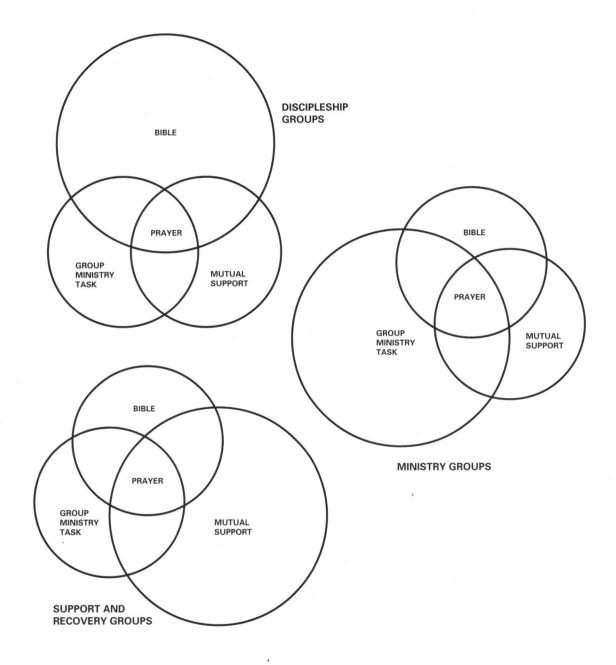

DISCIPLESHIP
GROUPS

BIBLE

PRAYER

GROUP
MINISTRY
TASK

MUTUAL
SUPPORT

BIBLE

PRAYER

GROUP
MINISTRY
TASK

MUTUAL
SUPPORT

MINISTRY GROUPS

BIBLE

PRAYER

GROUP
MINISTRY
TASK

MUTUAL
SUPPORT

SUPPORT AND
RECOVERY GROUPS

**Program Resource 1**

*Starting Small Groups—and Keeping them Going.* Copyright © 1995 Augsburg Fortress. May be reproduced for local use.

# Small group needs assessment

To help our planning team determine which small groups to establish, please complete the following interest survey and return it to the church office.

Check groups in which you have an interest.

## Support and Recovery Groups

- [ ] Parenting Young Children
- [ ] Sudden Infant Death Syndrome (SIDS) Support Group
- [ ] Single Parents
- [ ] New Parents
- [ ] Aging Issues
- [ ] Retirement
- [ ] Parents of Teenagers
- [ ] After Divorce
- [ ] Health and Nutrition

- [ ] Parents of Children with Special Needs
- [ ] Alzheimer's Support
- [ ] Mid-life Issues
- [ ] Unemployment Support
- [ ] Parents of Youth at Risk
- [ ] Divorced Women Over 45
- [ ] Teenagers Facing Difficulties
- [ ] Adult Children of Divorce
- [ ] Blended Families

- [ ] Grandparents Raising Grandkids
- [ ] Bankruptcy Recovery
- [ ] Adults Caring for their Parents
- [ ] Widows/Widowers
- [ ] Worshiping Alone
- [ ] Family and Friends of Gays and Lesbians
- [ ] Self-Esteem
- [ ] Communication
- [ ] Stress Management
- [ ] Infertility

The Twelve Step Process
- [ ] for Men
- [ ] for Women
- [ ] Parents and Tragic Loss
- [ ] Family Survivors of Suicide
- [ ] Adult Children of Alcoholics
- [ ] Abortion Recovery
- [ ] Victims of Sexual Abuse
- [ ] Grief and Loss
- [ ] Divorce Recovery

## Discipleship Groups

- [ ] Women's Study Group
- [ ] Men's Study Group
- [ ] How to Pray
- [ ] Basic Christian Beliefs

- [ ] Christian Families
- [ ] Small Businesses
- [ ] Marriage Enrichment
- [ ] Dealing with Doubts

- [ ] Christian Discipleship
- [ ] How to Study the Bible
- [ ] Discovering Your Spiritual Gifts

- [ ] Social Justice Issues
- [ ] Literature by Christian Authors

## Ministry Groups

- [ ] Helping the Homeless
- [ ] Prison Ministry
- [ ] Christmas Collections and Donations
- [ ] Ministry to AIDS Patients

- [ ] One-day Ministry Projects
- [ ] Food Shelf
- [ ] Shut-in Visitation
- [ ] Training/Skill Development

- [ ] Altar Guilds, Ushers, Greeters
- [ ] Choir, Musical Groups
- [ ] Teachers
- [ ] Council

- [ ] Committees
- [ ] Social Service or Advocacy Groups
- [ ] Food Service
- [ ] Special Event Planning Groups

Name _____    Phone _____

*Starting Small Groups—and Keeping them Going.* Copyright © 1995 Augsburg Fortress. May be reproduced for local use.

Program Resource 2

# 2 Studying Your Church

## First steps

With a planning team selected and assembled, it's time to begin working. The first steps include:

### Agendas

By planning your agendas to include prayer, biblical reflection, community building, and the task at hand, the planning team experiences the key small-group components: prayer, mutual support, biblical reflection and ministry task. This moves small groups from a concept to an experience that the team can naturally advocate.

### Practice

As planning team members become familiar with the components of healthy small groups, encourage members to try them in the church groups of which they are already a part—the altar guild, the social ministry committee, the men's fellowship breakfast.

### Multiple meetings

Plan on a series of meetings to properly analyze and evaluate information.

### Reading and research

Use various parts of this resource for background information, such as "Part 1: Understanding Small Groups" and Part 2, Chapter 1, "Building a Foundation." Refer to the books and articles in the "References" list (page 136) for additional background information.

Begin with these basics so everyone starts with the same foundation of facts and terminology. Then move to the next step, gathering data.

## Gathering data

Answering the question "Who are we as a church?" will assist your planning team in determining which approach to small group organization best fits your situation. Take some time to study and discuss the factors that might affect the development of your small group emphasis. Stages of development and implementation are directly affected by the following:

### Church size

In his book entitled *Sizing Up a Congregation for New Member Ministry,* Arlin J. Rothauge defines active membership as the worshiping and participating community and defines church sizes in the following way:

**The family church:** Up to 50 active members; the usual context is rural areas with some urban areas and small towns.

**The pastoral church:** 50 to 150 active members; the usual context is towns and suburbia.

**The program church:** 150 to 350 active members; the usual context is larger towns, urban, and growing suburban areas.

**The corporation church:** 300 to 500-plus active members; the usual context is cities and metropolitan areas (page 5).

No church size is better than another, but each will organize small group development differently. In a smaller church, the pastor may be responsible for most of the initial planning where in a corporation church, a volunteer lay leader or other staff member might do that. Also, smaller churches might choose to start one group and keep that going. The good news is that small groups work in any size church.

## Church characteristics

Church characteristics vary according to size and location. Characteristics to consider and discuss include:

- Staffing
- Annual budget
- Lay leadership potential
- Geographic personality
- Education levels of members
- Income levels of members
- Baptized membership
- Confirmed membership
- Number of family units
- Ages of members and of church
- Resource support for leaders
- Worship style (traditional, contemporary, other)
- Community demographics
- General attitude of membership (willing to grow spiritually and in numbers, to change, to risk)

## Cultural trends

George Barna, in *What Americans Believe*, addresses the characteristics of the U.S. population, including "baby boomers" (people born between 1946-1964) and "baby busters" (people born between 1965-1977). These groups represent two generations that generally have lifestyles, needs, and learning styles that present new challenges and opportunities for churches.

Baby boomers are thought of as the consumer generation. They are church shoppers and want choices. They work hard and expect a lot from a church. Baby busters, young adults presently in their 20s, most value career-related matters and having close friends; they value money and religion least. But as busters look to their future, only good health and living comfortably are more important to them than a close relationship with God. For boomers, only good health and being known as a person of integrity are more important than a close relationship with God. Fewer than half of boomers and busters strongly agree with the statement that "the Christian faith is relevant to the way they live." Boomers are more likely than busters to join a small group (pages 153-154, 166, 182, 265).

Age groupings are not the only way to look at cultural trends. In *U.S. Lifestyles and Mainline Churches*, Tex Sample discusses three groups he labels the cultural right, the cultural middle, and the cultural left (pages 4-5). The cultural right are people who live primarily in rural or town and country area. They value family above all else. Small groups need to enrich their family life and fit around their schedules of family commitments. The cultural middle seeks success and status. Small groups will need to prove to this group that it is worth their time and effort. The cultural left searches for meaning in life. Small groups need to meet this need for meaning, otherwise the members of the cultural left will be off to new spiritual ventures.

## Current and future small groups

Consider the following questions:

- Is our approach to organization of small groups independent, accountable, specialized, or integrated (see Chapter 1, pages 13-14)?
- What types of groups does our church have? Where do they fall within the descriptions of discipleship, support and recovery, ministry, or another combination?

Survey church members to learn what needs and priorities they identify. Use the needs assessment form provided on page 17 (Program Resource 2).

The organizational choices affected by the above data include:

- Setting a goal for your ministry through small groups. Do we remain the same or change our small group approach?
- Deciding who will develop this aspect of ministry. Will it be volunteers, existing staff, or new staff?
- Choosing a method of introduction. Do we add a single category such as support and recovery groups without changing the existing organizational structure of our church (specialized approach)? Do we start specialized small groups with the intention of moving gradually towards an integrated approach? Do we start new specialized small groups and assist existing small groups in changing to incorporate the key components of small groups (integrated approach)?

# Evaluating established programs

Make a list of all the groups in your church that presently meet on some regular basis. Include in this list who leads the group, when the group meets, and why the group meets.

Sometimes small group components can be integrated into existing groups. As you study this list, review the following questions to determine if any existing program, committee, or group would accept a small group orientation:

☛ Has this program or group always been a part of your church's history? Has this group had a long-established meeting agenda?

☛ What percentage of people participate, start, and finish the program or group? What is the ongoing attendance as it relates to church membership?

☛ Are the leaders and participants expressing excitement and satisfaction or fatigue and lack of interest?

☛ Are leaders and participants expressing a need for change, new ideas, new methods?

☛ How have new programs and ideas been introduced in the past? Can we learn from these experiences?

☛ What are the possible obstacles? Be realistic.

# Examining the programmatic year

The church's programmatic year presents both challenges and opportunities. When considering the introduction of a small group emphasis, review the following:

☛ Does existing programming (Sunday school, fellowship activities, social ministry projects) start and stop at predetermined times?

☛ What are seasonal busy times? For example, in many churches the busiest times are Thanksgiving to Christmas and Lent through Easter.

☛ When is church members' attention at its highest? For example, in many churches peak attention times are September after a summer break, January through March after Christmas and before Easter, and after Easter and before summer vacations.

☛ What major community festivals, events, and programs detract from participation levels in church activities?

☛ Consider the public school calendar: beginning and ending dates of the school year, winter and spring breaks, holidays, graduations, and other activities that affect the commitments of members.

Do introduce new ideas at opportune times, when people are more likely to participate. Don't introduce new ideas when people are personally or programmatically distracted.

# Reviewing options for meeting places

Small groups have many options for meeting places. The following represents a general guideline for types of groups and appropriate meeting places:

**Private homes.** Many discipleship groups find the congenial atmosphere of home meetings conducive to their gathering.

**Church building.** Support and recovery groups might be more comfortable with the anonymity of the church facility. Meeting at church also protects hosts from the potentially difficult situation of group members who show up at their door seeking additional support during non-meeting times.

Ministry groups (task oriented) often find the church facility more convenient should they need records or supplies to complete their agenda.

**Other locations.** Some groups find restaurants, bowling alleys, social service agencies, and parks workable alternatives.

Remember, a small group meeting need not be limited to the church facility.

## Speaking a common language

Local cultural orientations affect churches. Choose terms for your small group effort that will be received in a positive manner. Consider the following examples:

☛ Will support and recovery groups that are called "care groups" be confused with a community drug rehabilitation program called "The Care Unit"?

☛ Will the term "cofacilitator" to describe the person who assists the small group facilitator be more acceptable if called an "assistant facilitator"?

☛ Will the sports terms "coach" and "team" be more appealing than "facilitator" or "coordinator" and "group"? Or will they put off those who don't follow sports?

☛ Will terminology cause this new emphasis to be confused with a past effort that was not well received?

☛ Is there a present term for new member sponsors, such as "shepherd," that might be confused with discipleship groups called "shepherd groups"?

The connotations and nuances of language are different to each church. Use what is appropriate to your theological tradition and works best for you.

## Considering a budget

An allowance for your small group emphasis in the annual church budget gives a visible sign of support by church leadership and acceptance by members. Items to consider include:

☛ Staffing: Will we start with volunteers or the existing staff supplemented by volunteers? When do we anticipate the need to increase paid staff?

☛ Research information: Will there be fees for demographic studies and postage fees for needs assessments?

☛ Resources: What books, periodicals, training seminars, videos, or tapes may be needed to enhance small group growth and development?

☛ Supplies: Developing facilitator manuals, job descriptions, and needed forms will require paper and duplicating and postage fees.

☛ Planning meetings and ongoing organizational meetings might call for a refreshments allowance.

When your planning team has evaluated organizational approaches, the data it has gathered, established church programs, the church's programmatic year, meeting place options, terminology issues, and budget needs, you are ready to move ahead to the implementation stage.

# Chapter 3
# Implementing Small Groups

## Modeling small groups

Experiencing small group components is essential to developing support for and understanding of small groups among church members. Learning by experience is more effective than learning by hearing someone's opinion. This experience may indicate the intentional small group approach that will best serve your church.

Modeling helps a church experiment with different ways of organizing small groups. Modeling helps you do a language check. What terms seem acceptable? There are three possible methods of modeling.

### Create a new small group

A planning team member might serve as the small group facilitator, training a cofacilitator to take over leadership once the group is developed, or a planning team member might choose to set up all positions and remain part of the group but not act as facilitator.

**Advantages:** A new group accepts new organizational principles, components, and format more easily; new participants might more readily consider themselves "pioneers" and part of the team evaluating this experience.

**Disadvantages:** Starting "from scratch" requires more organization efforts—setting meeting dates, determining length of meeting and topic, selecting participants and curriculum, and so on.

### Refocus an existing group

A planning team member introduces and explains small group components to an existing group. Missing components are added and existing ones are changed as needed. This person stays with the group until they have grown into the new approach.

**Advantages:** The basics are in place: meeting dates and times, location, participants, and so on. Some components of intentional small groups already may

be part of the group gathering: prayer, biblical reflection, mutual support, or ministry task. They can add missing components and intentionally become an official small group. An established group that is not running effectively may be willing to try something new.

**Disadvantages:** Established groups might not accept change at all. An established group might accept a new goal, but not want to change how they are presently operating.

In general, groups which are task oriented find difficulty in adding relational components such as prayer and mutual support. Support and recovery groups and discipleship groups, which tend to be more relational, have difficulty adding task components.

Turn to Program Resource 3 (page 27) for a list of ideas about how to incorporate small group principles into other groups. Also refer to the training material in Part 3 of this manual.

### Create a new small group and refocus an existing group

This method requires strong organizational skills on the part of the planning team member because that person will be working with two groups at the same time.

**Advantages:** This method gives a small group emphasis more visibility by involving a larger number of people and groups. More information is readily available to the planning team for evaluation.

**Disadvantages:** This method takes a large time commitment. This method requires full-time attention by the assigned leadership, whether volunteer or paid staff.

Remember, first attempts at establishing small groups may not be perceived as successful. Evaluate, suggest modifications, and keep going. Small groups work, but you must work small groups!

## Outlining an initial plan

By now, much material has been reviewed. Compile all information and form recommendations to include:

☛ The small group approach that best serves your church

☛ A purpose statement for the emphasis as it relates to the church's mission

☛ The steps to take to achieve your goal

☛ The estimated time frame in which this goal will be accomplished

☛ The financial resources that need to be part of the annual budget

☛ The person or persons who will develop the small group effort

☛ A projection of future leadership needs

## Presenting results to leaders

Leadership support is vital. Present the material with recommendations to your governing council or board and request their endorsement at this preliminary stage. Outline the steps that you will be taking and how the council will be kept informed. Indicate if there are other steps where their endorsement will be sought, such as following the modeling stage. Invite those who have experienced small group dynamics to give a testimony to how small groups enhance ministry. Encourage these leaders to join a small group.

Meet with present group leaders, such as committee chairpersons and teachers, to introduce the concept and enlist their support.

When presenting the recommendations to church leaders, explain small group components (prayer, biblical reflection, mutual support, group ministry task). Share sample agendas of all three types of small groups (discipleship, support and recovery, and ministry groups). See samples on pages 28-30 (Program Resources 4, 5 and 6). If you have chosen to integrate all existing small groups in your church, be alert to current group leaders that may be receptive to refocusing their present group. Use their receptivity as an opportunity to model different components of small groups.

## Evaluating the model group experience

Evaluation of the model small group experience provides valuable information on what to do and what not to do again. Learn from this experience and start another small group. Allow participants in the original small group to be facilitators of other small groups and continue to evaluate the process.

The planning team continues to evaluate the model small group and all subsequent small groups that have been started in this early phase. This ongoing evaluation provides a reading on how your church accepts the emphasis and helps to determine the small group approach that will best serve your church.

## Introducing small groups to church membership

Simply informing your membership about a new emphasis is not enough. Help them catch the vision. Consider the following options:

☛ Use all written forms of communication: weekly bulletins, monthly newsletters, memos to current group leaders. Make this information inviting and informative.

☛ Use word of mouth. All leaders can encourage others to participate in a small group experience. Personal invitations work better than open invitations in the worship folder or church newsletter.

☛ Messages from the pastor during worship services identify small groups as a priority.

☛ Affirm the small group gatherings that have been in place. Assure them that what they have been doing is important.

☛ Current group leaders that support and understand small groups can begin using small group components in existing groups. This increases awareness among church members.

☛ Meet with the leaders of existing groups to share with them the vision and the possibilities. Give them some specific examples and stories of people feeling cared for in small groups. Share what you want to happen and why.

☛ Suggest that some of those who lead these groups take part in the facilitator training sessions that are offered.

- Consider developing a logo for your small group emphasis. Use it on all printed material related to small groups. If you plan to use an integrated approach to small groups, present the new logo alongside your existing church logo for a time. With the approval of the necessary governance committees, gradually incorporate the two into a new logo.

## Finding facilitators

In the early stages of implementing small groups, look for potential small group leaders, or facilitators, in the following places:

- The planning team that evaluated and recommended small groups

- The administrative commission or board that endorsed the recommendations

- The model small group and subsequent groups

- A special group that has been selected and invited to be pioneer small group facilitators

Consider persons with the spiritual gift of organization that are willing to take risks. A commitment to serving God—both in attitude and time—is vital.

## Training facilitators

Training is essential to an intentional approach to small groups for the following reasons:

- Training emphasizes that your church recognizes the importance of small groups.

- Facilitators gain confidence and skills.

- Facilitators are less likely to burn out when they receive support through training.

- Ongoing training and support encourages accountability and affirms responsibilities.

- Small groups are more likely to remain healthy and grow.

### Training approaches

When refocusing existing groups or working with experienced group leaders:

- Provide complete training before these people officially begin as small group facilitators, or

- Provide training in stages. Offer an orientation that covers the vision for small groups in your church and introduces these leaders to the organi-

zational details of your church's small group emphasis, such as agendas and job descriptions.

- Ask facilitators to complete an evaluation form that asks for training needs.

- Set training dates and agendas by the needs expressed.

Current group leaders are already facilitating and may not be receptive to being trained. Many present or experienced group leaders respond best when the training is perceived as a need and not an obligation or extra meeting.

When starting new groups or utilizing inexperienced small group facilitators, consider the following:

- Provide complete training before a facilitator begins in a small group, or

- Provide an orientation that includes the vision for small groups in your church and sample agendas, suggested curriculum, job descriptions, and accountability procedures.

- Allow these potential facilitators to experience a small group already in progress.

- Allow these facilitators to begin a small group and complete an evaluation form stating their training needs.

- Set ongoing training sessions according to the established needs.

New facilitators may be more receptive to full training before they actually begin the small group. Ownership in the training increases response and participation.

When training facilitators, use the extensive training material found in Part 3 and the reproducible program resources in this section of the manual.

Consider the following additional information about small group facilitator training.

- When developing training sessions, start small. Offer training, support, or enrichment sessions once or twice in a calendar year. The next year quarterly, then monthly or weekly as appropriate.

- From the beginning, plan training thoughtfully and present small group concepts effectively or facilitators will not consider it important and attendance will suffer.

- Orient facilitators to the other personnel involved: cofacilitators and hosts. See the "Small Group Leadership Diagram" (Program Resource 7, page 31).

- Reinforce the vision of small groups for your church at all training sessions. Affirm the evolutionary development based on research and ongoing evaluation.

## Developing facilitator manuals

Developing a small group facilitator manual is essential to training and ongoing support of the facilitators and small groups. Small group facilitators need assistance in the care and nurture of the participants in their small groups. Having a written job description and forms for administrative tasks such as attendance, evaluation, and general record keeping help them in their efforts at care and nurture. See the sample job description, page 32 (Program Resource 8).

A facilitator manual also serves as a tool to support accountability. Small group facilitators serve in an important ministry of caring for people. Regular written reports submitted to a small group coordinator can help to identify weak spots where the group or facilitator needs help or refocusing. See Program Resource 9, page 33.

Use the following guidelines to select materials for the manual:

☛ Determine the most important administrative tasks and design those forms first. Possible forms include attendance, general information sheet on each participant, and a listing of responsibilities (host, prayer leader, study leader, child care coordinator, and others that a group can decide on).

☛ Add forms and enrichment material to the manuals as feedback from facilitators is assessed. Sections in a manual may include:

   ☛ sample agendas

   ☛ report forms

   ☛ how to order curriculum

   ☛ how to reserve a room in the church facility

   ☛ job description and accountability procedures

Do not overwhelm facilitators with forms. Do solicit input and develop forms as needed. Forms and organization should serve ministry, not hamper it.

Orienting small group facilitators to the manuals can happen in several different ways:

☛ Invite all facilitators to one meeting.

☛ Invite facilitators by small group type to one meeting. For example, all leaders of support and recovery groups could attend a meeting together.

☛ Visit small group facilitators individually.

In all settings, provide time for feedback, evaluation, and suggestions. Encourage ownership. A small group coordinator will need to supervise the use and ongoing development of these manuals.

## Finding coordinators

A healthy small group effort grows. How many small group facilitators can one person supervise? When does the number of small groups become unmanageable?

In his book, *Prepare Your Church for the Future,* Carl George outlines another tier of leadership, here called "coordinators," that expands the single staff person or volunteer's ability to care for a growing ministry of small groups (page 122). Customize this concept to meet the needs of your church (see the sample job description in Program Resource 10, page 34). Consider the following:

☛ Coordinators care for a set number of small group facilitators (suggested maximum is five).

☛ A primary staff person or volunteer supervises, trains, and supports the coordinators.

☛ This level of leadership may be organized by small group type such as coordinators for discipleship groups, coordinators for support and recovery groups, or coordinators for ministry groups.

☛ This level of leadership may be coordinated by teams. Example: Team A has ten coordinators who each care for five small group facilitators. The primary staff person or volunteer may train and support teams A, B, C, and so on.

☛ This level of leadership may be organized geographically.

☛ This level of leadership may be called coordinators, coaches, or any other name that appeals to your members.

☛ Successful small group facilitators who are willing to accept more responsibility are potential coordinators.

☛ A coordinator level of leadership established early in the development of small groups needs to be trained as small group facilitators and receive ongoing training and support.

## Scheduling alternatives

Consider these possible meeting schedules for discipleship and support groups, both ongoing and short-term groups.

### Alternative A

☛ Seven weekly meetings in the fall. This schedule can enable a group to develop close relationships and a commitment to each other. Schedule it so that the time between Thanksgiving and Christmas is relatively free. Groups can meet socially in December.

☛ Twice-monthly meetings from January until June.

☛ The summer months are more conducive to social gatherings involving families or significant others, but don't discourage those who want to continue regular meetings during these months.

☛ The fall can be a time to continue the twice-monthly groups as well as start up new groups that will meet weekly as they begin.

### Alternative B

☛ Meet weekly seven to ten times in the fall.

☛ Take a Christmas break.

☛ Meet weekly from January until Lent or Easter.

☛ Take a spring break.

☛ Meet weekly for six or seven sessions after Easter.

☛ Take a summer break.

☛ Start the cycle again.

### Alternative C

☛ Start the group off with a six- to seven-week beginning course that meets weekly.

☛ After a break, encourage each group to decide how frequently they will meet.

### Alternative D

☛ Some short-term groups might meet for four to six weeks, then stop.

### Alternative E

☛ Some groups might meet biweekly for three to six months.

### Alternative F

☛ Other groups might choose to meet weekly for two to three months.

## Marking the official beginning

Recognition affirms and establishes a ministry and its leaders as priorities. Consider the following:

☛ Plan a commissioning service for your small group facilitators and coordinators. Planning this as part of a worship service highlights this aspect of your church's ministry and sets these leaders apart for a special function. Most denominations have an order for the recognition of lay ministers or lay ministries, or both. Any of those services may be appropriate. See Program Resource 11 (page 35) for a sample service.

☛ Plan a dinner with a program that includes some of the small group components (prayer, mutual support, biblical reflection). The closing activity might be to commission the small group facilitators.

☛ Produce publicity flyers that announce and introduce the plan for small groups that your congregation has adopted. Distribute these flyers to the community by mail, community newcomers packets, or as door hangers.

☛ Create banners for the worship center that highlight small groups.

☛ Display your church's mission statement showing its commitment to small groups.

Once they are going, small groups need continuous attention to keep them going. The next chapter identifies key aspects of ongoing development.

# Small group components for leaders of other groups

■ Begin each gathering with a community building question and a time for bringing each other up to date. Some possible questions to use when you first start doing this are found in "LifeStories/FaithStories" (Training Handout 13, page 117).

■ Try to be aware of what's going on in the lives of each member so that when a special celebration or crisis occurs, others in the group can be informed and respond appropriately.

■ Include a brief time for devotion during each gathering, if you don't already do this. Encourage the use of Bible texts and take time to apply a thought from the text to the present context of life situations. Ask for the group's insights or questions. Use open questions, not those that call for one word answers.

■ Take time to pray together. Use prayer as an opportunity to include concerns and requests from the group members. Go around the circle and ask each person what they need God's help with at this time. An alternative is to rejoice together over answered prayers or recent blessings experienced through meditation or prayer.

■ Always take time to be available for each other. This can be experienced while performing a task or some activity together. It includes active listening, storytelling, and the art of asking questions.

■ Gradually move deeper in your community building questions, and allow more time for this component. Begin to ask feeling questions, as well as giving history or sharing facts. Give members the time and attention to become more open and honest about what's going on with them.

■ After your meetings follow up on people with personal attention to individual needs or questions. Ask various members to follow up with other people. Develop teams or pairs of people who can become closer as they work together.

■ When the opportunity presents itself, encourage members of your group to join a small group where the focus is loving and supporting one another. Be familiar with groups that are available and when they meet.

■ As a leader, continue to evaluate what is happening with your group of people, not only whether their task or activity is going well, but whether community is being experienced. Pray for this to happen.

*Starting Small Groups—and Keeping them Going.* Copyright © 1995 Augsburg Fortress. May be reproduced for local use.

## Purpose:

We trust the Holy Spirit to work through small groups to create a healthy church environment and give a renewed sense of belonging to each person, nurtured through fellowship around God's Word, prayer, and worship. Our purpose as a small group puts people first. If a need is expressed by a participant, we take time to support that person.

## Agenda (60- to 90-minute meeting):

1. Opening: 5-10 minutes

   ■ Introductions of visitors

   ■ Icebreaker

2. Biblical reflection: 10-15 minutes

3. Opening prayer: 2-5 minutes

4. Support and recovery content focus: 30-35 minutes

5. Group ministry task: 5-10 minutes

6. Sharing of prayer concerns: 5-10 minutes

7. Closing prayer: 3-5 minutes

## Format of meeting:

Each small group may alter the agenda order and total time of meeting to best suit the needs of your group, but all elements of small group dynamics (prayer, Bible, mutual support, group ministry task) are necessary for the group to remain healthy.

## Timing:

It is important that your small group understand the contract for your meeting time. This includes knowing that you will stick to the agenda and to the time commitment.

Program Resource 4

*Starting Small Groups—and Keeping them Going.* Copyright © 1995 Augsburg Fortress. May be reproduced for local use.

# Discipleship group agenda

### Purpose:
We trust the Holy Spirit to work through small groups to create a healthy church environment and give a renewed sense of belonging to each person, nurtured through fellowship around God's Word, prayer, and worship. Our purpose as a small group puts people first. If a need is expressed by a participant, we take time to support that person.

### Agenda (60- to 90-minute meeting):
1. Opening: 5-10 minutes

    ■ Introductions of visitors

    ■ Icebreaker

2. Opening prayer: 2-5 minutes

3. Discipleship content focus: 35-45 minutes

4. Group ministry task: 10-15 minutes

5. Sharing of prayer concerns: 5-10 minutes

6. Closing prayer: 3-5 minutes

### Format of meeting:
Each small group may alter the agenda order and total time of meeting to best suit the needs of your group, but all elements of small group dynamics (prayer, Bible, mutual support, group ministry task) are necessary for the group to remain healthy.

### Timing:
It is important that your small group understand the contract for your meeting time. This includes knowing that you will stick to the agenda and to the time commitment.

Program Resource 5

## Purpose:

We trust the Holy Spirit to work through small groups to create a healthy church environment and give a re-newed sense of belonging to each person, nurtured through fellowship around God's Word, prayer, and worship. Our purpose as a small group puts people first. If a need is expressed by a participant, we take time to support that person.

## Agenda (60- to 90-minute meeting):

1. Opening: 5-10 minutes

   - Introductions of visitors
   - Icebreaker

2. Opening prayer: 2-5 minutes

3. Ministry content focus: 30-35 minutes

4. Group ministry task: 5-10 minutes

5. Sharing of prayer concerns: 5-10 minutes

6. Closing prayer: 3-5 minutes

## Format of meeting:

Each small group may alter the agenda order and total time of meeting to best suit the needs of your group, but all elements of small group dynamics (prayer, Bible, mutual support, group ministry task) are necessary for the group to remain healthy.

## Timing:

It is important that your small group understand the contract for your meeting time. This includes know-ing that you will stick to the agenda and to the time commitment.

Program Resource 6

*Starting Small Groups—and Keeping them Going.* Copyright © 1995 Augsburg Fortress. May be reproduced for local use.

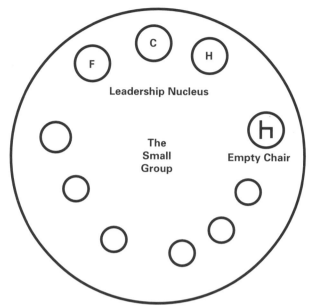

F = Facilitator who is trained to lead

C = Cofacilitator who may lead a group in the future

H = Host whose home is used or who arranges the use of facilities elsewhere

ℏ = Empty chair as reminder that the group is open and welcomes others

Circle = A reminder that the small group is a face-to-face gathering. People interact best when they are able to face each other, see each other, and hear each other. The circle reminds us that each person is valuable and there is no hierarchy or dominate leader.

**Program Resource 7**

*Starting Small Groups—and Keeping them Going.* Copyright © 1995 Augsburg Fortress. May be reproduced for local use.

# Job description: facilitator

The small group facilitator is the person who is appointed and recognized to serve as the leader of a group by enabling the members to achieve their purpose for being a group.

**Qualifications:**

- Previous participation in a small group
- People person, relationally oriented
- Positive attitude, nonjudgmental
- Effective communication skills
- Spiritually and emotionally healthy
- Integrity (honest and reliable)
- Committed to Christ and an active church member
- Teachable
- Good sense of humor
- Has a desire to serve

**Responsibilities:**

- Attend all training sessions for facilitators
- Interview with the pastor or small group coordinator
- Be a team member with all the other facilitators
- Recruit or help find a cofacilitator
- Attend follow-up meetings of facilitators
- Promote small groups in the church
- Pray for the small groups and each member of your group

Program Resource 8

*Starting Small Groups—and Keeping them Going.* Copyright © 1995 Augsburg Fortress. May be reproduced for local use.

# Facilitator report form

Facilitator: Please fill out this form as often as instructed by the small group coordinator and return it to the coordinator.

Facilitator name: _____

Date: _____

Small group name: _____

Location of meetings: _____

Frequency of meetings (circle one):

weekly                    bi-monthly

monthly                   other _____

Total number of group members: _____

Cofacilitator name: _____

Host name:_____

## Attendance report:

How many were present? _____

Date: _____     Number: _____

Date: _____     Number: _____

Date: _____     Number: _____

Date: _____     Number: _____

Who was absent? (Include dates and names.)


Absentee follow-up:

__ by telephone

__ by mail

__ other: _____

## Visitors and new group members:

Note address and telephone number if they are not members of the church. We want to keep in touch.

Date:                          Name:

_____          _____

_____          _____

_____          _____

_____          _____

## Group health

Is the small group healthy? Comment on strengths and weaknesses.

## Essentials

Comment on your success at covering these four essentials:

☛ Prayer

☛ Biblical reflection

☛ Mutual support

☛ Ministry task

## Special concerns of group members:

☛ What facilitator training topics would be helpful?


☛ How long will your group continue?


☛ Will you continue as group facilitator?


☛ Other comments:

*Starting Small Groups—and Keeping them Going.* Copyright © 1995 Augsburg Fortress. May be reproduced for local use.

# Job description: small group coordinator

## Summary:

The small group coordinator oversees and coordinates a specified number of small group facilitators and their groups so that they will be able to successfully achieve their group purpose.

## Qualifications:

- The ability to explain the small group vision
- The ability to work well with others
- The ability to encourage a facilitator who needs encouraging, confront a facilitator who needs confrontation, and guide a facilitator who needs guidance.
- Timeliness (being able to collect required forms and data in a regular and dependable manner)
- Knows when someone in a group needs referral
- Listening skills
- Thorough knowledge of group dynamics
- Positive, encouraging attitude

## Responsibilities:

- Champion our small groups.
- Monitor the health of the groups through personal interaction with facilitators, report to the small group director or pastor, and periodically visit the group.
- Encourage and guide facilitators in their own growth.
- Help and train facilitators to find their cofacilitators and develop them. Assist facilitators in starting new groups as cofacilitators develop and the need arises.
- Meet with facilitators during any future training opportunity.
- Supervise the choice of content and application of group materials along with the pastor.
- Help group facilitators deal with persons who are difficult. Help them decide when to refer such people to support groups or other resources.
- Submit reports on the progress of each of the group facilitators being supervised to the small group director; keep the small group director abreast of strengths and problems in the group.
- Monitor group participation in ministry projects and outreach efforts.

Program Resource 10

*Starting Small Groups—and Keeping them Going.* Copyright © 1995 Augsburg Fortress. May be reproduced for local use.

# Commissioning service

**Placement in service:** The commissioning of small group facilitators may appropriately be placed after the Offering and the Offertory in the worship service. Some service books offer suggestions regarding other appropriate placements within the service.

---

*The pastor addresses the congregation:*

Dear Christian friends: Baptized into the priesthood of Jesus Christ, we all are called to offer ourselves to the Lord of the church in thanksgiving for what God has done and continues to do for us. It is our privilege to recognize and support those who are engaged in the ministry of this church, especially those involved through small groups.

*A representative of the congregation reads a brief description of the ministry to be recognized; the persons engaged in that ministry are called to the altar.*

Scripture reading:
*(Possible texts include Romans 12:4-8, 1 Peter 4:8-11, Matthew 20:25-28)*

*The pastor addresses the persons before the altar.*

P: Will you assume these responsibilities of ministry in our church in the confidence that they come from God?

**R: I will, and I ask God to help me.**

P: Will you trust in God's care, seek to grow in love for those you serve, strive for excellence in your skills, and adorn the gospel of God with a godly life?

**R: I will, and I ask God to help me.**

P: Having offered yourselves as small group facilitators in this church, will you follow Jesus' example of humble service?

**R: Yes, with God's help.**

P: Let us pray.

O God of love, your Son washed the feet of his disciples as a sign of servanthood. Uphold those who follow his example of humble service, and strengthen them in their faith. Help us all to do faithfully those deeds of love and mercy expected of your servants; through Jesus Christ our Lord.

**R: Amen.**

P: For all who offer themselves in your name, we give thanks, O God. Give them joy of service, and constant care and guidance. Help us all to be both willing servants and thankful recipients of ministry, that your name be glorified, your people live in peace, and your will be done; through Jesus Christ our Lord.

*Those at the altar may return to their seats. The service continues with the offertory prayer.*

Excerpted from "Recognition of Ministries in the Congregation" (pages 143-145) and "Installation of a Lay Professional Leader" (pages 137-138) in *Occasional Services: A Companion to Lutheran Book of Worship.* Copyright © 1982.

**Program Resource 11**

*Starting Small Groups—and Keeping them Going.* Copyright © 1995 Augsburg Fortress. May be reproduced for local use.

Chapter

# 4 Ongoing Development

## Promoting small groups

Ongoing promotion and information sharing about small groups helps church members get on board. The majority of your church's members will need time to hear, absorb, and process information about small groups before they respond with active support and participation.

As the emphasis gains support, use existing programs and events to further introduce small group dynamics and help members experience the benefits of small groups. Members who experience small groups will be more likely to join small groups. Options include:

### Annual stewardship

Organize an every-member visit with small groups meeting in members' homes. Model small group components.

### Adult Sunday school

Present a large group study and then break into small groups for discussion highlighting the relational (prayer and mutual support) aspects of small groups.

### Worship service

Plan worship to fit a theme related to small groups, one that highlights the benefits and the biblical basis for this expression of ministry. In bulletin inserts, include explanations of small group components (prayer, biblical reflection, mutual support, and ministry task) and illustrations that show how existing small groups fall into different small group categories (discipleship, support and recovery, and ministry groups).

### Confirmation

Present material in large group sessions to confirmands and break into small groups with adult small group leaders to process the information and build relationships.

### Fellowship activities

Organize small groups for reflection on Scripture and prayer.

### Service tasks

Include prayer and a reflection on Scripture before the group leaves to complete its task. In larger groups break into small groups to pray before or after the task, or both.

### Small group fair

Ask small groups to set up booths with posters, illustrations of activities, representatives with whom to speak, and refreshments.

Think of new and creative ways to say the same thing. Repetition is necessary to reach all members and potential members, as well as to keep the vision alive and well.

### Additional possibilities

☛ Affirm facilitators and coordinators by verbal and written methods.

☛ Report total attendance in small groups on a weekly basis in your worship folder.

☛ Celebrate during a special Sunday morning fellowship time the first time a group multiplies into two groups.

☛ Celebrate the start of all new groups.

☛ Publicize all training sessions with details of the agenda to increase awareness and interest. Extend an open invitation to anyone who is interested in learning more about small groups.

☛ Have facilitators and coordinators wear special name tags or buttons identifying who they are and their small group leadership roles.

- Produce T-shirts or caps with the church logo and small group emphasis theme. Make them available to leaders and participants to wear weekly or on designated Sundays.

- Periodically present information during worship services or hear testimonies from participants who have had positive experiences in a small group.

- Create a small group directory and keep it updated and available for reference. Give new members a copy when they join the church.

## Inviting the wider community

Small groups serve as outreach into the community. Consider the following:

- Methods for sharing information include local community newspapers, brochures as door hangers, brochures in local businesses, radio announcements, and individual member invitations.

- Be alert to community needs and establish groups with the express intent of inviting the wider community.

- Establish classes (not small groups) and invite participants to join a small group that continues after the class ends. A class format that begins and ends may be more appealing to nonmembers and serve as a bridge to involvement in small groups.

- When beginning this specific outreach effort, use more experienced small group facilitators and have an administrative structure established. This increases the chances of nonmembers having a positive experience within the church.

## Increasing the number of small groups

You can increase the number of small groups sponsored by your church in three ways: by starting new groups, refocusing new groups, and multiplication.

### Starting new groups

New groups can be perceived as exciting and accepted with enthusiasm by both facilitators and participants. New groups are easier for people to join because everyone is new. Review your small group needs assessment survey (see page 17) to establish new groups in the needed categories. Those who indicated an interest in a particular group or topic can be called when the group is established.

Your planning team may have recommended one type of small group, such as support and recovery, to start with. Add groups to provide varied groups within the category.

As you add groups, remember that you will need to recruit and train facilitators and publicize the start of the new groups.

Ask church staff to recommend potential participants and provide a personal invitation if confidentiality is not an issue.

Provide several ways for people to join a small group:

- By calling the church office

- By contacting the small group facilitator

- By completing forms inserted in the newsletter and weekly worship folder

- By sign-up sheets posted on an announcement board

### Refocusing existing groups

Another way to increase the number of small groups is by refocusing existing groups. You might start with groups that have a purpose similar to the type of small groups you have already started, such as a men's Bible study group. Invite them to consider some changes.

The next time the men's Bible study group meets, encourage the leader to take time at the meeting's beginning to have everyone share how it's going in his life and pray together. See Program Resource 3 on page 27, "Small Group Components for Leaders of Other Groups."

Groups in the church that can be refocused or shaped to reflect the small group emphasis might include:

| | |
|---|---|
| Choirs | Staff meetings |
| Work groups | Travel seminars |
| Committees | Women's groups |
| Sport groups | Planning groups |
| Councils/boards | Bible studies |
| Task forces | Ushers |
| Sunday school teachers | Altar guilds |

Change is challenging and people may resist. Proceed at a slow pace. Introduce small group dynamics one at a time.

Celebrate and recognize a group that refocuses successfully to the small group orientation. This will encourage other groups attempting the same changes.

## Multiplication

A third way to increase the number of small groups is by multiplication. Small groups that are healthy will eventually reach a capacity of ten to twelve participants. To retain its effectiveness, it is important to keep the small group small. The group may multiply into two groups by having several participants, including the facilitator or cofacilitator, leave the original group to launch a new group.

Once a small group bonds it is sometimes difficult for multiplication to take place because it is seen as division—the group perceives that it is splitting up—which has a negative connotation. Include education about the process of multiplication in facilitator training and in introductory publicity to the church. With proper education and time, the concept may be accepted and some groups will be able to successfully multiply.

Recognize groups that successfully multiply so that the process is affirmed and other groups are encouraged to try.

This process is further explained in *Prepare Your Church For The Future* by Carl George (see "Resources" on page 137 for further information).

## Increasing participants in small groups

You can intentionally increase the number of participants in small groups in several ways. All groups should be considered open to newcomers, except in the case of some extremely sensitive, personal issues (for example, a support group for those who have been sexually abused).

One way to keep this goal of openness before the group is to have an empty chair present at each meeting. Generally the group is publicized as being open to new people at all times with an empty chair waiting to be filled. An intentional effort is made at praying for an empty chair to be filled in that group.

Ask facilitators to encourage current participants to invite and bring new members to the small group and to ask the staff for suggestions of persons to invite. Then ask them to recognize visitors and new participants in all small groups.

Distribute the inactive list of the church membership rolls to facilitators. Ask them to pray for those on the list and extend invitations.

## Encouraging leadership development

Future facilitators or coordinators can be developed from existing small groups. Encouraging leadership skills helps participants identify and use their spiritual gifts for ministry. Feelings of affirmation and usefulness will help keep participants connected to the group and to the church.

☛ Ask small group facilitators to identify a cofacilitator from within the group. This person is a "facilitator-in-training." (See Program Resource 12 on page 40.) A cofacilitator may become the leader of a new group that multiplies from an existing group or may become the facilitator of another new group.

☛ Delegation of other tasks include:

**Host** (see Program Resource 13 on page 41)

**Prayer leader**

**Bible study or devotion leader**

**Child care coordinator**

**Activity coordinator**

☛ Recognize and celebrate the many gifts of small group participants. Highlight one group a month in the newsletter and list all participants and their leadership roles.

# Evaluation

Ongoing evaluation of your small group effort at frequent and varied intervals will guide its continued development and strengthen your efforts. Consider the following:

☞ Distribute written evaluations to small group facilitators and participants. (See Program Resources 9 and 14 on pages 33 and 42.)

☞ Review attendance patterns in small groups.

☞ Assemble key leaders, perhaps the small group planning team, periodically for group discussion of some of these questions:

What comments are being shared by church members?

What is the general attitude of the church toward small groups?

Is the terminology we have chosen helping or hindering our efforts?

Is the chosen organizational approach working in this church?

Should we consider moving from one organizational approach to the another?

Is our communication, promotion, and marketing working? Should we increase our efforts?

Are negative experiences a result of moving too fast?

What report forms are working? What forms should be dropped or developed?

Is training of leaders effective? Should numbers of training sessions be increased or decreased?

Is the empty chair concept being utilized in small groups?

Is leadership being developed from within the small groups?

How far have we progressed in our projected evolutionary process of developing small groups?

# Job description: cofacilitator

The small group cofacilitator is the person appointed to assist the small group facilitator in leading the members of the group so that together they will fulfill their group objectives.

**Qualifications:**

- Listening
- A team player, does not need to be in charge
- Committed to the ministry of small groups
- A willingness to learn
- Understanding of small group purpose and process
- Ability to ask for help if needed
- Interested in talking to people about small groups
- A people person

**Responsibilities:**

- Attend regular meetings of the group.
- Promote the concept of small groups and help recruit participants.
- Help prepare for the meetings as assigned by the facilitator.
- Fill in for the facilitator when needed.
- Meet with other facilitators when asked to do so and attend training opportunities.
- Meet with facilitator to discuss the group.
- Pray for participants in the group.

Program Resource 12

*Starting Small Groups—and Keeping them Going.* Copyright © 1995 Augsburg Fortress. May be reproduced for local use.

# Job description: host

The small group host arranges for a group meeting place.

**Responsibilities:**

- Offers place of residence or arranges for the use of a public place for the group meetings. The group may decide to move from place to place after the first few meetings.

- If needed, prepares a map to the meeting place and sees that every participant can easily find how to get there.

- Prepares the meeting area with chairs in a close circle and not more than two persons on a sofa. Removes objects that hinder eye contact between all members. Sees that proper room temperature is maintained.

- Works with the group facilitator in providing a warm welcome to people as they arrive. Makes everyone feel comfortable.

- Arranges simple refreshments to be served when the facilitator decides to have them served. Finds out from facilitator who will bring refreshments at subsequent meetings.

- Works as a teammate with the facilitator and cofacilitator in creating a positive, cheerful, and supportive atmosphere.

- Prays for the group participants, appointed leaders, and the health of the group.

Program Resource 13

Please fill out and leave with your facilitator. Thank you.

1. Our small group has been of help to me in building relationships.

| 1 | 2 | 3 | 4 | 5 | 6 | 7 |
|---|---|---|---|---|---|---|
| A lot | | | | | | Little |

2. The biblical reflection has helped us listen to God's Word and connect it to our lives.

| 1 | 2 | 3 | 4 | 5 | 6 | 7 |
|---|---|---|---|---|---|---|

3. The curriculum has been helpful.

| 1 | 2 | 3 | 4 | 5 | 6 | 7 |
|---|---|---|---|---|---|---|

4. Our small group facilitator(s) led the group well.

| 1 | 2 | 3 | 4 | 5 | 6 | 7 |
|---|---|---|---|---|---|---|

5. Facilities, organization, and details were well handled.

| 1 | 2 | 3 | 4 | 5 | 6 | 7 |
|---|---|---|---|---|---|---|

What has been surprising to you?

What has been the most difficult or new to you?

What suggestion would you make for improvement?

The person from our group that I'd suggest as a small group facilitator in the future is:

How many of the sessions did you attend?

Other comments:

Signature (optional): _____

*Starting Small Groups—and Keeping them Going.* Copyright © 1995 Augsburg Fortress. May be reproduced for local use.

# Integrating New Members

# Chapter 5

## Churched and unchurched

Small groups provide multiple points of entry into a church. With an increasing number of unchurched people in the general population, we cannot always assume that a worship service will be the first experience a nonmember has with a Christian community.

Churched and unchurched persons have different priorities, which affect the way they integrate into a church. Consider the following characteristics of each.

### Churched people

☛ Usually have prior denominational experience, which may be positive or negative

☛ May have denominational loyalty

☛ May consider a specific organizational approach important and question change

☛ May favor traditional forms of small groups: Sunday school classes, committees, Bible studies

☛ May financially support the overall ministry of the church including ministry beyond local causes

☛ Usually begin integration into the church by attending worship services

☛ Frequently seek a personal relationship with the pastor

### Unchurched people

☛ May have no prior church experience

☛ Usually have no denominational loyalty

☛ Usually are concerned with effectiveness and efficiency of organization and are usually looking for a church that offers diverse opportunities to meet specific needs

☛ May be more accepting of non-traditional approaches that emphasize relationships

☛ Usually will financially support specific ministries that are closer to hame

☛ May connect to a small group before they attend worship services, with support and recovery groups being the most popular type of small group

☛ Are not necessarily seeking a personal relationship with the pastor

## Small groups and new members

New members need assistance as they begin or continue their faith journey within a new church. Healthy small groups are excellent opportunities for new members to integrate into the church.

Organization of the new member integration process requires intentional efforts by an assigned committee, a volunteer coordinator, or a staff person. In a small church, a pastor frequently organizes the process and delegates specific tasks. As you work to integrate new members, consider the following ideas.

A new member class is usually the first small group experience a new member has in your church. Develop a new member class that models small group components: prayer, biblical reflection, mutual support, and ministry task. The number and length of these classes can vary but a guideline might be a minimum of four one-hour sessions. In a large new member class (more than twelve people), break into small groups for part of the meeting. The content of these sessions can also include basic denominational beliefs and an orientation to the church (organization, leadership model, and facility design). The leader of the new member class is often the pastor but can be another designated staff person (or lay leader).

If the meeting time is prior to or following a worship service, have new members wear name tags and join the other worshipers after or between services for fellowship. Is there a regular fellowship time that would be better? This time provides another way to emphasize the importance of relationships.

Select sponsors for family units or individual persons. Define how you expect them to relate to new members.

Use an inventory to identify the new members' spiritual gifts. This information can be used to connect new members to small groups, among other things, and gathered in one of several ways: as part of the new member class; in a meeting apart from the new member class; in individual sessions by appointment.

As part of the information provided about your church, distribute a written directory of opportunities that includes all small groups and their facilitators to new members. A separate section might list specific tasks within the church. This resource for marketing and promotion is especially helpful for new and potential new members.

After new members have been received into membership, offer a second small group experience. This gathering serves as a bridge into a more active role in the church. This experience helps new members integrate at a more comfortable, individual pace and encourages people to care for people. Sponsors of the new members might also participate in this class. Other church leaders and members may be introduced at various times during this class further exposing the new members to more people in a less threatening environment.

Other possible content includes:

☛ Focus on God's plan for using spiritual gifts. The inventory may be completed as part of this class.

☛ Use curriculum for discipleship groups and build stronger relationships and commitment to serving God.

• • • • • • • • • • • • • • • • • •

**"New people in a church tend to search out new groups in which they can establish relationships of sharing and caring."**

Kennon L. Callahan, *Twelve Keys to an Effective Church*, page 36.

• • • • • • • • • • • • • • • • •

Review the results of the inventory and, following the class, be ready to connect people to an appropriate small group by spiritual gift(s) or present need(s) (or both). One way is to encourage the facilitator to invite the new member. People who are task oriented may prefer a ministry group; people who are interested in spiritual growth may prefer a discipleship group; people who are experiencing a trauma in their life may prefer a support and recovery group.

At the completion of this second new member experience, the small group coordinator, new member coordinator, or pastor arranges to have the new member invited to an existing small group meeting without asking for a commitment to join immediately. This method of introduction builds another bridge from new member class to existing small group.

Small groups that are open and that fully understand the empty chair concept will warmly welcome new members. Some small groups that are unwilling to follow your church's small group approach will not be healthy places for new members. Make certain that small group facilitators receive a complete orientation to the new member process.

The new member or small group coordinator monitors the new member placement. If the initial placement is not working, that person helps the member find a new small group. If all parts appear to be working and the person is not connecting, the coordinator refers that person to the pastor or follows up with a personal contact to determine the reasons.

For a new member to feel a part of the church's ministry takes about eighteen months to two years. This may vary by size and location. Effective small groups strengthen the process of integration.

# Ten Cautions

## Caution one: Moving too quickly

Most people perceive change as a loss and, therefore, a negative experience. Taking time to model a new concept, develop support, and build positive experiences increases the chance that the initiative will be more readily accepted than one that is dictated as law. Incremental change offers better comfort zones for church members. Do not attempt too much, too soon.

## Caution two: Failure to customize

Churches need to be flexible and intentional about developing small groups that strengthen their ability to minister. One organizational approach to a small group emphasis will not fit every situation.

## Caution three: Keeping groups part of the system

Small groups can believe that they are self sufficient and attempt to become independent of the larger church. They may choose not to worship with the community. Monitoring the health of small groups with a strong leadership structure reduces the chances of this happening.

## Caution four: Involving key leaders in the process

If a church does not own the effort, the level of development will be greatly limited. Involving key church leaders along the way strengthens trust and support of the effort.

## Caution five: Sensitivity to established structures and programs

Whenever possible, introduce change as an addition instead of a subtraction; as a positive instead of a negative. Start new small groups or refocus existing small groups that have broken parts in their structure.

## Caution six: Involving the staff

Changing the church's style of ministry can be threatening to the existing staff. Pastoral support and participation is imperative from the start. Other staff job descriptions might change and they too need to be kept informed and involved. A fully integrated system of small groups affects all members of the church's professional staff.

## Caution seven: Training and nurturing facilitators

Giving facilitators opportunities for skill building will avoid frustration, burnout, and a sense of failure. Leaders develop leaders; take care of them.

## Caution eight: Evaluating regularly

Periodic checks are important to evaluate progress and effectiveness. "Is this working?" and "How can we do this better?" are questions that need to be asked frequently. Revisit your original goals and objectives. Are they still valid?

## Caution nine: Communicating with membership

Education through constant communication with church members is essential. Repetition is a valid form of education: Find new ways to say the same thing. People who are aware and informed can be supportive.

## Caution ten: Perseverance and prayer required

Don't give up the first time you hit a roadblock. Challenge is part of change and change provides opportunities for growth. Learn from mistakes and keep going.

In whatever we undertake, we can easily lose our way and become obsessed with process, technique, and results. Seek guidance and strength from God through prayer and reflection.

## Conclusion

Developing ministry through small groups is a journey that will provide challenges, successes, and failures. Keep moving forward, turning failures into learning opportunities, understanding and expecting change to take time, and recognizing that our salvation does not depend on our church's structure or ministry.

An intentional, relational model of small groups will work in any size church and in a variety of ways. In the words of Dale Galloway, "It is a matter of creating ministries that meet people at the point of their need and helping people to become disciples and grow into producing disciples" (quoted in Elmer L. Towns, *10 of Today's Most Productive Churches,* page 86). A journey into small groups that recognizes people's need for support and growth in a Christ-centered community will be successful.

# 3

# Training Small Group Facilitators

# Introduction

Pastors and lay staff discover that small group facilitators become their primary assistants for pastoral ministry. Time spent in recruiting, training, and keeping in touch will reap many benefits for the staff and for the entire church.

The suggestions in this section of the manual are provided for pastors or small group coordinators who do not have extra time to do the kind of study and research they may want to do. The following assumptions guided the writing of this training material:

☛ Your church leaders and other members own the decision to have small groups and to do the job well.

☛ Small groups fit into the mission of your church.

☛ Facilitators will serve best if given training.

☛ An experience of community is important and needs added attention in your church.

☛ The trainer has a basic understanding of biblical and gospel-centered theology.

☛ The trainer is willing to be creative and discerning in the use of this material.

☛ The size of your church and the number of groups you will start with will determine how best to adapt this material.

☛ Small groups are important and vital to ministry, but do not need to do everything or cover all aspects of the church's ministry.

At some point in your training sessions, you may want to go over these assumptions with your trainees and add others that may be true for you.

## The need for training

People asked to facilitate small groups need to receive adequate training and encouragement. Those who try short cuts in this process are usually inviting frustration or defeat in the long run. Asking people to facilitate small groups without training can result in:

☛ Difficulty in finding volunteers to lead groups

☛ Groups that don't have proper understanding of their purpose or goals

☛ Inadequate supervision of what happens in the groups

☛ Ruining the reputation of small groups in your church

☛ Giving facilitators the impression that what they are doing isn't important

☛ Lack of proper organization or promotion time for a small group emphasis

Starting fewer small groups with trained facilitators is more wise than having many groups with facilitators who are not trained. Even those trained in small group leadership skills elsewhere should be encouraged to renew their skills and become part of the community of small group facilitators in your church. Those committed to being facilitators become leaders in pastoral ministry in the church.

## Training overview

The training material that follows focuses on learning the dynamics of small groups and developing the various skills needed to facilitate a group. The general purpose of the training sessions is to help small group facilitators:

☛ Understand how small groups fit into the overall mission of the church and connect us to God's created order and purpose in creation

☛ Learn the components of a healthy small group—biblical reflection, prayer, mutual support, and ministry

☛ Define their own leadership characteristics, qualities, and styles and develop skills in leading a small group

☛ Experience what enables relationships to develop

No two churches are alike. No two persons read material with identical interpretation or appreciation. As the trainer, use what is helpful in this training material and adapt it to the people and community you work with. Become familiar with the material in Chapter 7, "About Training Facilitators," and Chapter 8, "About Small Groups," prior to your first training session. Decide the key points you want to share with facilitators.

Chapter 9, "Training Sessions," contains information to guide you as trainer through each training session. The material for the first five training sessions in this book is useful for facilitators of all types of groups: discipleship, support and recovery, and ministry. Additional instruction for those asked to facilitate support and recovery groups is provided in Session 6. General group dynamics and leadership skills apply no matter what the group's type or purpose is, but support and recovery groups can present some unique situations for participants and facilitators.

You can train ministry group facilitators using the material in this section and by following the methods described in Part 2. See Part 2, Chapter 3 and Program Resource 3 (page 27) for information about adding the four components to existing committees and other task-oriented groups.

Part 3 concludes with a brief description of an agenda for ongoing facilitator training

The training handouts found on pages 97-135 are reproducible for you to distribute to the facilitators being trained. You might provide three-ring binders for facilitators in which to keep their training handouts, report forms, job descriptions, and the like. See the section on "Developing Facilitator Manuals" (page 24) in Part 2, Chapter 3 for more ideas.

Many people have contributed to the insights and discoveries that are shared in these chapters. Refer to the "References" and "Resources" lists on pages 136-138 to learn more about those who have done pioneer work in the area of small groups.

# Chapter 7

# About Training Facilitators

## Small group leadership roles

What should we call the persons who are trained to lead a small group? In this manual they are called facilitators for three reasons:

1. The word *facilitator* describes what the people do. They monitor and encourage the group to do its work. A facilitator is at the service of others in the group. Small groups need to know that each member, not only the leader, is responsible for the group's success.

2. The title *facilitator* is less threatening than the term *leader* to someone who may be inexperienced. Recruitment is easier when the term facilitator is used.

3. At times a facilitator needs to lead. However, the word *facilitator* does not connote the person who holds all control, authority, and expertise. Small groups function best when they do not see their facilitator in this role.

Arthur Baranowski, in his book *Creating Small Faith Communities,* calls the leaders "pastoral facilitators" (page 81). There is something to be said for this title. Pastoral ministry happens in small groups. The title helps the person to be linked to the parish and reminds us that we belong to a priesthood of all believers. Pastoral facilitators are pastoring the church with the pastor. The small group they lead is a community where people experience church. The caring that takes place is a pastoral function. This title may raise questions for those who want to reserve use of the word pastor for ordained professionals. Whatever word is used in your setting, choose it with care and then explain it to those who will hear it used.

Other important participants in small groups are the cofacilitator and the host. The cofacilitator assists the group facilitator and is often in training to become a small group facilitator. The host offers his or her place of residence for the group meeting or hosts the meeting at a public place. Detailed job descriptions for the facilitator, cofacilitator, and the host can be found in Program Resources 8, 12, and 13 (pages 32, 40, 41).

## Facilitators—called, trained, appointed

### Called

Small group facilitators are usually volunteers who respond to an invitation from a pastor or other leader in the church. There are two aspects to their calling. One is the inner sense of being called by God to use their gifts for this particular aspect of ministry in the church. This calling seldom comes with fanfare or visions, but more often with a feeling that there is a need and a call from God to fill that need. The other aspect of the call comes when a church leader asks the volunteers to seriously consider being small group facilitators. This might begin with an invitation to attend the training sessions. Volunteers may also experience a calling when friends see in them the skills of a small group facilitator (see Training Handout 6, page 110, which lists some of these skills).

### Trained

Churches that take seriously the power and potential of small groups will take seriously the importance of training their small group facilitators. Past experiences will be part of that training. Potential leaders are often found in existing groups. People who have taught Sunday school or served as youth counselors or discussion leaders will find their experiences helpful. Some may even have taken a college class in communication or speech. But more is needed. Facilitating small groups requires special training.

### Appointed

When one senses a calling to be involved in this part of a church's ministry, and has taken time to be trained, the next step is to be appointed. This includes a confirmation by the pastor or appointed leader that the volunteer is ready to begin facilitating a group. Some persons will go through the training and decide not to facilitate a group. This need not be looked upon as a defeat or failure. The volunteer's training can make them even more supportive in any group they join.

How facilitators are appointed varies. They might be asked to organize their own group. There may be a group all ready to go. The appointment celebrates the training the facilitators have received and recognizes the work they will do. Publish the names of group facilitators and/or have a prayer of consecration or commissioning service on a given Sunday as part of the appointment process (see "Marking the Official Beginning," Part 2, Chapter 3 (page 26) and Program Resource 13, page 41).

## Support of group facilitators

To keep small groups going in a church once the effort is underway facilitators need to be given support, direction, and encouragement. The staff person responsible for small groups needs to make a commitment to the facilitators that they will not be forgotten or neglected once they are meeting regularly with their small group. That commitment includes:

**Keep in touch.** Let the facilitators know you support them with mailings, home calls, and words of affirmation.

**Continue skill training.** On the job training will improve the facilitator's effectiveness.

**Develop a leadership community.** Facilitators need a support system outside their own groups.

**Review and renew the vision.** Leaders need inspiration. Stimulate their imagination and motivate them.

## Regular meetings with facilitators

Part of the commitment to serve as a facilitator should include a willingness to attend monthly or regular meetings of all small group facilitators led by the pastor or small group coordinator. Find a time to meet that will make it possible for everyone to come. If your small group effort is large enough, you could provide two choices, but then you lose some of the sense of community when not all are together for this time.

Build your meetings around these principles:

☛ The facilitators need encouragement and affirmation.

☛ The facilitators have experiences to share and will learn from each other.

☛ The facilitators have problems and questions they need to ask.

☛ The facilitators become a community that needs nurture and development.

☛ The facilitators need continued skill training. Not everything was covered in the initial training sessions.

☛ The pastor and other staff need to know what's happening in the groups and be encouraged in pastoral ministry.

☛ The pastor and staff coordinator need to give guidance to the overall ministry.

☛ The pastor or staff coordinator needs to keep the facilitators informed about church events and scheduling.

☛ The pastor needs to give theological guidance to the facilitators.

## Appointing small group coordinators

It becomes difficult, sometimes impossible, for one pastor or lay staff person to give proper attention and encouragement to each small group facilitator. This becomes even more true as your ministry through small groups expands and diversifies. Build into your long-range plans a time to appoint overseers or coordinators of a small number of small group facilitators. (See also Part 2, "Organizing Small Groups in Your Church.") These coordinators should be small group facilitators themselves and have the respect of other small group facilitators. They become responsible to keep in touch with the facilitators assigned to them, make sure they are listened to, and answer their questions.

At the regular gathering of all small group facilitators, coordinators gather with their facilitators at the appointed time for sharing and prayer. The number of persons assigned to each coordinator may vary. Four or five may be a way to start. The pastor or other person responsible meets with all the coordinators and thereby keeps informed of what's happening in all the groups. See the job description for coordinators in Program Resource 10, page 40.

Small group facilitators will find support from each other. They will become a community themselves. Encouragement will come as they share experiences and struggles. Their monthly meeting with the pastor or coordinator will give them opportunities to learn from each other, be renewed, and pray for each other.

# Learning from others

There is no need to go it alone in beginning or continuing a small group emphasis. Your ideas and plans will improve with a teachable attitude. Be open to learning from others. You don't have to agree with everything in another approach in order to examine it for new ideas. Here are some ways to learn from others:

☛ Be alert to members of your church who have taken college courses in small groups or who teach communication skills.

☛ Look over textbooks that are used at the college level for classes on small groups.

☛ Watch for workshops or conferences that deal with small group development. If you can't attend, send a representative from your church. Include funds for this activity in your next year's budget.

☛ Check with your denominational offices to see what networking is available in the area of small groups. Start a network.

☛ Exchange materials with others who are using something they find helpful. Ask around at pastor's gatherings. Be inquisitive.

☛ Ask about what is new in the small group movement in other denominations. Look for ideas on promotion, training, study guides, and follow-up.

☛ Have a conversation with someone from Latin America who is experienced in base Christian communities. See what can be learned from them.

☛ Explore what is being learned about the relationship between healing and small groups, the discovery of gifts and small groups, the stewardship of money and small groups, or church growth and small groups.

☛ One may be surprised by exploring what some of the church fathers and mothers have said that relates to small groups. Luther and Wesley are positive examples. Study the Hauge movement in Norway or the pietistic movement in Germany. Go back and reread *Life Together* by Bonhoeffer, *Taste of New Wine* by Keith Miller, *Call to Commitment* by Elizabeth O'Connor, or *The Reconstruction of the Church—On What Pattern* by E. Stanley Jones (see "Resources," pages 137-138, for more information).

☛ The house church movement in North America has a close connection to what small groups are about. They have a newsletter called *Voices*. The Roman Catholic church has a good newsletter on small groups called *Buena Vista Ink*. For information on obtaining these newsletters, see "Resources" (page 138).

☛ In your devotional reading of the Bible or related books, be alert to texts that relate to the place of community, the ministry of building each other up, and caring for one another.

# About Small Groups

Chapter 8

## Small groups and communication

Communication is vital to small groups. Communication includes relationship building, self-expression, listening, being listened to, receiving, feeling, and speaking. As you think about training facilitators, consider the following ideas about communication:

☞ God communicates with us. God speaks to humanity in more than one way. The use of Scripture provides small groups with God's Word. God also speaks to small groups as participants communicate with one another.

☞ God created humans to communicate. As social beings we are made to express ourselves in order to live together, grow together, and serve together. We become more human as we learn to communicate and receive communication.

☞ We communicate with God. As small groups pray, they speak to and listen for God. Small groups also communicate their feelings to God as they share, study, and work together.

☞ Community dies without communication. Alienation, loneliness, fear, and feelings of rejection happen when we don't communicate. Suffering and various kinds of pain result when we live in isolation.

☞ We are strangers without communication. Unless we take the effort to express ourselves to one another we never really know one another. Small groups encourage communication and provide a place to welcome the stranger.

☞ Love is communication. Love is not a doctrine or theory. It is an experience. We express and experience love through our specific acts of communication.

☞ Communication is sometimes nonverbal. Messages are sometimes transmitted through touch and facial expression as well as words. Because groups gather in intimate, face-to-face settings, nonverbal communication is possible.

☞ Being present to someone is communication. Small groups allow us to be present to one an-

other and our presence communicates a willingness to listen, learn, and love.

☞ Listening is communication. Most people long to be listened to. When they sense we are really listening, they receive a message from us that we care. A relationship grows.

☞ Encouragement is communication. We all need affirmation. Small groups enable us to encourage each other in ways that might not happen otherwise. Gifts are discovered and encouraged through communicating.

☞ Storytelling is important communication. Everyone has stories to tell. They help us to examine and change our lives. Small groups give permission for storytelling.

☞ Communication needs testing. Small groups provide the space, time, and setting to allow participants to check to see that they are hearing correctly, that the message is clear, and that their listening is not distorted because of a bias or barrier.

The subject of communication is covered in Training Session 3, "Mutual Support." Also see Program Resource 10 (page 34).

## The small group covenant

The group covenant or contract provides the key to good small group communication. A group covenant is a shared agreement of the purpose of the group, what the participants want to accomplish, and the responsibilities required of each participant. As trainer, you will introduce this concept to the facilitators in Training Session 4. A sample covenant that can be used as a guide in developing your own is available in Training Handout 16.

Some basic items that need to be covered in a group covenant are:

☞ Regular attendance: Participants need to give priority to the group.

☞ Participation: Everyone is responsible for a successful group.

- Confidentiality: A sense of trust is important.
- Openness: Participants will be honest.
- Prayer: An agreement to pray for one another.
- Support: Give permission to ask for help.
- Ministry: Agreement to put the good news into action.
- Growth: Seeking to grow in discipleship and service in following Christ.

## Confidentiality

One of the most important elements of the covenant is confidentiality. For trust to develop within the group, participants need to agree that what is shared in the group stays in the group. There may be times when someone may ask for permission to share another participant's disclosure outside the group and does so only with permission, but the general rule of confidentiality must prevail.

Confidentiality is important because a caring community only develops where truth is spoken and upheld with the assurance that it will be accepted and kept in confidence. The participants' freedom to be honest and open grows out of an atmosphere of love and trust.

When the group covenant agreement is discussed at the beginning of the group's formation, the element of confidentiality needs to be clarified, but not with such force or legalism that participants are frightened. Make it clear that to maintain an atmosphere of love and trust everyone is asked to keep the things shared in the group in the group. A failure to do this will hurt the whole group.

The group facilitator will want to find ways to remind the group of the covenant of confidentiality. The covenant might be reread periodically. Occasionally an illustration may be used to point out the importance of trust and how intimacy grows out of trust. The group can be asked to pray for openness, trust, and honesty.

Of course there will always be the risk that someone may break the confidence. It will be impossible to monitor what people do between sessions. There is some risk involved whenever we establish meaningful relationships. When confidentiality is broken and it threatens to damage the group, the facilitator should talk to the persons involved and seek to restore a healthy atmosphere. If necessary, involve your pastor.

## Meeting frequency and group longevity

### Meeting frequency

When deciding the frequency of small group meetings consider these three questions:

1. What is your group's purpose?
2. What is feasible?
3. What has worked in your church in the past?

In order to build relationships and community, groups need to meet frequently. If a group meets only once a month, that might be too long a time between meetings to stay connected, remember last meeting's conversation, or sense progress in feeling support and encouragement. Because participants lead busy lives, weekly meetings may not be a possibility. For these reasons many groups opt for biweekly meetings or two meetings and a social outing each month. More people are likely to commit themselves to a small group for as long as a year if they know it will require only two meetings a month. For sample schedules, see "Scheduling Alternatives" in Part 2, Chapter 3 (page 25).

### Group longevity

Most people find that participation in a group is most fruitful when they stay together at least two years. At the outset two years may seem like a long commitment to many people. For this reason it is a good idea to ask initially for shorter commitments that are renewable. Persons just starting out in a small group may need to have a taste, a beginning experience, before they commit to a longer involvement. If participants have the option to withdraw at various points, small groups will attract more persons and will reduce the practice of sporadic attendance.

Consider this schedule:

- Begin with a commitment of six to seven sessions, meeting weekly or twice a month.
- After a break, commit to twelve months or another specified amount of time.
- Continue to renew for twelve months at a time.

# Why small groups need to remain small

There is not a hard and fast rule for how many people should be in a group. In Exodus 18, Jethro advised Moses to break the multitude down into groups of ten. Small group proponents recommend groups of seven to twelve for maximum effectiveness. If a small group has fifteen or twenty persons attending, their gathering may be good and useful but it is not a small group.

A key component of a small group is mutual support. Many people don't feel cared for or valued until someone has heard them. It is difficult to listen effectively to a hundred voices or even twenty voices. Be very cautious about letting groups get larger than twelve.

Another important element of Christian nurture and growth is the permission and encouragement to share one's struggles, one's feelings, one's dreams, and one's questions. In a group of more than twelve, participants have less time to share and respond. The feeling of being timed or rushed can stifle honest sharing.

A more subtle problem with groups larger than twelve is the temptation for some to hide in the crowd. Rather than talk about one's life in relation to the Christian faith, a person lets others talk. The very person who needs to participate may shy away from it because others so easily do the talking.

A practical matter is the role of the facilitator. Responsibly monitoring and encouraging balanced participation is a big task. Twelve people is about all one facilitator can adequately lead, despite the fact that all the participants are responsible for the group's interaction.

In using seven to twelve as a general goal for small group size, remember that on certain occasions there will be someone absent. If too many are absent, participants might want to reschedule the meeting. Encourage them to be careful so that this won't become a habit. A loyalty to the group is a must for the group to effectively minister to one another.

# Life cycle of a small group

Most small groups progress through various stages: the birthing stage, the maturing stage, and the termination stage. Between and during these stages there are periods of struggle and ecstasy. Facilitators need to be aware of these stages in group development, and recognize signs of sickness or wellness and act accordingly. When it is evident that a small group has reached the end of its useful life span, the facilitator helps the group terminate gracefully.

Signs to look for in the life cycle of a small group are:

## The birthing stage

- Not everyone is sure they want to be committed to the group. Some may be asking, "Is it worth my time?"

- Participants don't know each other well, even if they have known each other for years.

- Some compare this new small group with other Bible studies or groups in which they have participated.

- Ideas and suggestions come mostly from those who are more talkative in groups. Silent ones may have ideas but not share them out loud.

- The facilitator may appear nervous at first and be tied to the agenda or the written material rather tightly.

- Participants want to be assured they will not be embarrassed and that the meeting begins and ends on time.

- Answers are often short and deal more with facts than with feelings.

## The maturing stage

- Intentional community-building activities are still needed but not quite as much time is spent on them.

- Participants follows up on what's happening in each other's lives.

- The use of humor increases and participants feel more free to laugh and expose their weaknesses.

- Answers expose deeper feelings, doubts, and questions. Participants do not feel the need to appear strong.

- If the facilitator misses a point or makes a mistake, others bring it to his or her attention.

- Growth and change in people's lives become more evident.

- Application of the Scriptures for daily life becomes more personal.

- Dissatisfaction with the group's progress may become more easily shared by the participants.

- Ministry tasks become more important as people begin to see the importance of being doers of the Word.

- Leadership rotates more easily and the group becomes less dependent on the facilitator, though a facilitator is still needed.

## The termination stage

- Attendance slacks off. Excuses for missing seem to demonstrate less commitment to the group.

- The group becomes ingrown.

- Participants get into a rut of intellectualizing rather than applying what is learned to daily life, and efforts to correct this do not succeed.

- A negative attitude toward the church or toward the group experience prevails. The same negative single issue or personal complaints surface again and again.

- Personality clashes begin to hinder growth or prevent caring from taking place and the participants seem unable to make any progress in dealing with them.

- The church is at a point where a change is needed in small group makeup. The life of the church calls for a shift.

- A written evaluation by the group reveals enough signs that it is in the best interest to terminate the group while positive feelings about small groups still exist.

For a list of examples of when groups terminate see "Why Groups Terminate," Training Handout 32. See also Training Handout 33, "How to Gracefully Terminate a Group." This material will be covered in Training Session 5.

## Limitations and risks

Small groups have received popular press. Church leaders tell stories of how small groups are transforming their churches. Some will throw themselves into a small group emphasis with everything they have, hoping to solve longstanding problems or barriers to growth and spiritual renewal. Some caution is in order. There are certain risks involved. Some of the risks and limitations of small groups are listed below:

1. Small groups do not take the place of corporate worship and the need for celebration by the whole body of Christ.

2. For various reasons some church members will not get involved in small groups no matter how well they are promoted. A pastor and others need to minister to these people as well. They are not second-class Christians.

3. Church staff and volunteers have only so much time to fulfill all the tasks that need attention. To take on planning and supervising small groups will mean sacrificing other tasks. Churches cannot add programs without also letting go of other programs and activities.

4. Small groups can become cliques or gripe sessions if not carefully facilitated. Some participants are looking for a place to complain or spread rumors.

5. Some groups can promote a god that is foreign to the God we know from the Scriptures. A theology can develop in a group that may not be consistent with the teachings of the church.

6. Feelings and relationships become important if not primary in the experience of community. Sometimes too much emphasis can be placed on feelings, especially in communities where there has been a lack of opportunity and encouragement to talk about feelings. For these people, expressing feelings is too overwhelming or turns them off.

7. When one partner is involved in a small group without the other it may result in jealousy, conflict over time and scheduling, and a breakdown in their communication. In some situations, the partner who is attending the group may form an unhealthy relationship with a group member.

8. Small groups can become a threat to the other programs already in place. People may neglect other commitments because they find the small group meets so many personal needs.

9. Small groups should not become an excuse for neglecting marriage and family relationships. On the other hand, it is appropriate for adults to take care of themselves and not neglect their own needs.

10. Some groups just do not work. Sometimes the mix of people or other circumstances prevent the development of a healthy sense of community.

11. Occasionally, facilitators will not be able to fulfill their responsibilities. Some facilitators will be better suited to one group over another. Others may prefer assisting or participating in the group.

12. Small groups do not give people a comprehensive knowledge of the Bible. People in small groups don't learn to know the individual books of the Bible as they would in a Bible class. Content is not primary in small groups. A church needs to offer other opportunities for this kind of Bible knowledge.

13. Many people who have been long-time members of a church have not been taught about giving priority to community through mutual support. They have not been encouraged to tell their stories and share their struggles. In some cases seminary training has not adequately prepared pastors for building community. These churches and pastors may be initially resistant to a small group emphasis.

Small groups are needed. The Holy Spirit can work through them to do wonderful things for the church. Without them we miss an important opportunity to meet the needs of those seeking Christian community. But they will not solve all our problems. The content of the training sessions that follow reflects the benefits and limitations of small groups.

# Training Sessions

## About the training sessions

### Four components

The training of small group facilitators emphasizes the four components of each session or gathering. The names given to these components may vary but the general content is similar. As you prepare for the facilitator training and begin to examine various resource material, keep in mind these four parts of each group gathering.

1. **Biblical reflection** is a part of small group gatherings. Depending upon the type of small group, biblical reflection may be the group's main focus or simply a brief devotional time that begins a task-focused meeting.

2. **Mutual support** or community building happens through intentional activities, discussion, and informal ways members "connect" with each other. As the group gathers, various activities enable the members to relax and feel comfortable with each other. As the group moves into its time of reflection, mutual support develops as personal stories and insights are shared. A caring community is built and strengthened as group members work together on common ministry task.

3. **Prayer** binds the group to God and to each other. Most small group gatherings begin and end with prayer, which may take on a variety of forms.

4. **Ministry task** refers to outward-directed service that group members undertake together. Some groups make this their primary purpose. All types of small groups can benefit from putting their experiences and discoveries into action on behalf of others.

### Sample guide

In Training Handout 1 you will find a sample chapter from *Following Jesus: Encouragement from the Beatitudes for a Troubled World* (Augsburg Fortress, 1995). This material is included as a working tool for learning about a small group focused on Bible study. If possible, the trainer should have a copy of the 64-page resource, which contains six chapters.

The trainer should read over this sample in advance to become familiar with its flow and its various components. During the facilitator training sessions, there will be an opportunity to use a designated part of the sample as an exercise in practicing what is being discussed. Remember, not all study guides on the market are arranged as this one, but it gives a taste of what to expect and how material facilitates the group process.

## Options

The material presented for training facilitators is usable in a number of settings or models. It is possible to present it in fewer sessions or expand it to include more time together. To do so the trainer will need to become familiar with the various sections and find ways to adjust it without losing the full impact. Some assignments can be made for completion between sessions, but the best learning will happen while in session with others, through discussion, and on-the-job training. Well-trained facilitators will be some of the best promotion of small groups in your church.

## Schedule

When you begin your training sessions you will want to have a tentative agenda and timetable in mind so that you can do justice to the entire lesson. When no agenda is planned, trainers often come to the end of the lesson of the series and discover that important things are left out. If you pick and choose among the various components and material available, do so intentionally, not for lack of planning.

A general schedule for your leadership training may look something like this:

| | |
|---|---|
| **Welcome, introduction, biblical reflection, and prayer** | **10-15 minutes** |
| **Community building and gathering (may be less in later sessions but always include)** | **20-30 minutes** |
| **Content focus** | **30-45 minutes** |
| **Questions, review, and preview of next week** | **10-15 minutes** |
| **Closing** | **5-10 minutes** |
| **Total** | **75-115 minutes** |

# Session one: the small group facilitator

## Outline:
- Prayer
- Community building exercises
- Scripture lesson
- Introduction to small groups
- Biblical and theological foundation
- Four basic components of small groups
- The small group facilitator
- The facilitator's job description
- Discovering leadership styles
- Review and questions

### Materials needed
- General materials: Bibles, pens or pencils, writing paper, chalkboard and chalk or newsprint and markers.
- Training Handouts (one copy of each handout for each trainee): 1, 2, 3, 4, 5, 6, 7
- Program Resources 7, 8, 12, 13

### Preparation:
- For the exercise under "Introduction to Small Groups" (page 62), make an extra copy of Training Handout 4. Circle the important words and phrases in each definition. Cut up the definitions so that each word or phrase is on a separate slip of paper.
- As background to "Biblical and Theological Foundation" (page 63), reread Part 1, "Understanding Small Groups."

## Prayer

Begin with a prayer, thanking God for the trainees.

## Community building exercises

### Sample session guide

**1.** Turn to Training Handout 1. Inform trainees that you will be going through the various parts of this material at different sessions.

**2.** Work through the first two "Community Building" questions and the option. Under the second question, each person could choose one of the three questions.

**3.** Note:

☛ The questions were the kind that almost everyone could answer. They didn't require certain educational background, religious experience, or profound analysis.

☛ It is important to give people options when first asking for group participation.

## New experiences

**1.** Ask the group of trainees to think of an experience they have had when they were in a new place, a new group, or a new circumstance. It might have been a first class, a new church they visited, starting a new job, a first date, or a first performance.

**2.** Ask them to respond to the following questions.

- ☛ What was it like?

- ☛ How did you feel?

- ☛ What ran through your mind?

**3.** As the group responds, record their answers on chalkboard or newsprint where everyone can see. You may want to add to the list or suggest thoughts or feelings that are common to first experiences.

**4.** With the list completed, ask an additional question:
What kind of things helped or would have helped you feel more secure in that situation?

Some answers that often surface are:

- ☛ Being noticed, not rejected, not treated as an outsider

- ☛ Somebody knowing my name, calling me by my name

- ☛ Knowing what to do next, where to go, where to sit

- ☛ Sensing that someone is in charge and knows what's going on

- ☛ Understanding instructions, expectations, and options available

- ☛ Someone asking me a question that enabled me to let them know who I am

**5.** Ask the group to keep these things in mind as they think about people coming to a small group for the first time.

## Pairs

**1.** Ask the group of trainees to pair off, preferably with someone they do not know well.

**2.** Instruct the trainees to tell their partners about themselves. Ask, "What could you share in three minutes to help that person know you better?" When time is up, tell the trainees to switch roles.

**3.** When each pair has finished, ask the trainees to join with another group. Instruct the trainees to take turns introducing their partners to the new group.

**4.** When all four have finished, ask them to discuss the following in their groups of four. Ask one person to write down the responses to the second question.

- ☛ What were your immediate feelings when you were asked to find a partner? What did you think? Were you afraid?

- ☛ What kind of help would be most useful for you in this series of training sessions for small group facilitators?

**5.** After a few minutes call the whole group together and have them report on the kinds of help they are looking for.

> The small group
>
> movement is a quiet
>
> revolution taking
>
> place in today's soci-
>
> ety that is altering the
>
> way we view God and
>
> relate to one another.
>
> Robert Wuthnow,
> *Sharing the Journey.*

## Scripture lesson

**1.** Explain that the use of the Bible in small groups will be a main focus for Session 2, but that at each gathering you will include some reflection on God's Word as it relates to small groups.

**2.** Read Acts 2:41-47 and instruct trainees to discuss the statements provided in Training Handout 2.

**3.** Ask the trainees to connect the text to small groups. Or ask, "Where do you find yourself in this Scripture text?"

(Not all texts need to be used. You will find these passages useful at various stages in the training process.)

## Introduction to small groups

**1.** Give a brief history of small groups in your church, affirming what has been done and lifting up the vision for the future.

**2.** Tell a real-life story of how someone's life has been transformed through small groups. This could be from your own experience or a story someone has told you.

**3.** Distribute and review Training Handout 3, "Benefits of Small Groups."

**4.** Ask the trainees to share with the group experiences they may have had with small groups. Their experience may be church related, work related, or community related.

### Definitions

**1.** Ask the trainees to look at Training Handout 4, which lists three definitions used by different churches.

☞ The concept of small groups is used widely today and many definitions are applied.

☞ There is no one correct definition of small groups. However, there are elements that most small groups have in common.

☞ In these training sessions the first definition will be used. If you have chosen another one or developed one of your own, let the facilitators know.

**2.** After the trainees have looked over the definitions, break into groups of three people.

**3.** Distribute the slips of paper containing the important words and phrases from the three definitions.

**4.** Ask each group of trainees to pantomime their word or give a sentence description. The others can guess what important element of the definition the group was assigned.

## Three elements for community

**1.** Present the following to the facilitators:
If a primary goal of small groups is to provide a place where people are individually encouraged, supported, and loved, then three elements will become extremely important.

- ☛ Small groups are a place to be heard: It is vital that the group listens and that each participant feels listened to.

- ☛ Small groups are a place to be accepted: The group needs to be reminded not to stereotype or prejudge people because of their age, marital status, level of spirituality, sexual orientation, or personal viewpoints.

- ☛ Small groups are a place to feel cared for: The group becomes a source of support for each participant. This support might range from a practical and physical level (hospital visit, transportation, food, or physical labor) to a more inward level (prayer, counsel, affirmation, accountability). Both levels are a form of spiritual care.

**2.** Discuss the following questions.

- ☛ Reflect on the difference between listening to someone and the person actually feeling like he or she has been listened to. How would you describe the difference and what can be done so that the person feels listened to?

- ☛ What are some indicators that a judgmental attitude is present in a group? How can a facilitator handle a situation when nonacceptance is being felt or expressed?

- ☛ What is it about small groups that enables people to care for each other in ways that don't often happen in large gatherings? Ask the facilitators if they can name ten people in their church who pray for them personally on a regular basis. That can happen in a small group.

## Biblical and theological foundation

**1.** Explain briefly the foundation for small groups found in the Bible. Use the following outline, which is based on Part 1, "Understanding Small Groups":

- ■ History provides examples of ministry through small groups
  Old Testament examples
  New Testament examples
  Church history examples

- ■ Criteria for healthy small groups:
  Small groups listen to God
  Small groups are caring places
  Small groups relate to the church
  Small groups welcome the stranger

**2.** Let the trainees know that in the next session considerable attention will be given to the scriptural foundation and the use of the Bible in small groups.

3. In this session you might touch on some of the points listed below:

☛ Creation itself supports the need for people to relate to people. We are created as social beings. God made us to live in relationships.

☛ The Hebrew scriptures (Old Testament) is a story of how God worked within a community. The Israelites were divided into groups in various ways. The individual was always seen as part of a group, and responsible to and for others.

☛ The experience of community has been central to the mission of God's people throughout history.

☛ Jethro's advice to Moses, who was leading the Israelites through the wilderness, included dividing the masses into subgroups, the most numerous being a group of ten (Exodus 18:13-27; see also Part 1).

☛ Jesus ministered through a small group of both men and women. Jesus himself needed the support of a small group (Luke 8:1-3).

☛ An important step for Jesus in the healing process was giving voice to the one hurting, to self-expression (Luke 8:43-48). In small groups people dare to disclose their pain.

☛ The early church was a community of communities. They were house churches where it was possible for caring and sharing to happen (Acts 2:42).

☛ We are called to love one another (Romans 12:10) and bear one another's burdens (Galatians 6:2). Passages that use the phrase "one another" will be looked at in the next session.

4. After you have gone over these biblical and theological foundations, write the words below on a chalkboard or newsprint.

| | |
|---|---|
| **Creation** | **Jesus' example** |
| **Old Testament history** | **Giving voice to the poor** |
| **Mission** | **House church** |
| **Jethro's advice** | **Called to love** |

5. Ask the trainees to choose one and then relate a story, an example, or an illustration of how this aspect of our Christian heritage points to the importance or practice of ministry through small groups.

## Four basic components of small groups

1. Turn to Training Handout 5 and review the four basic components of small groups with the trainees (prayer, biblical reflection, mutual support, and group ministry task).

2. Explain the following:

These four elements may be called by different names and they may be emphasized to varying degrees. It is these elements, however, that make a small group a small group. In the sessions that follow, attention will be given to at least one of these elements. There will be an opportunity in the training sessions to practice the components with one another.

# The small group facilitator

**1.** Present the following to the group:

No one is more vital to the success of a small group than the leader whom we call the facilitator. Most people who will consider the possibility of being such a small group facilitator will have some questions and apprehensiveness. Am I really qualified? Will I be able to handle it? Isn't there someone better qualified? I don't want to be a leader but I'll assist.

It's good to remember that there is no perfect small group facilitator. We are all continuing to learn and we are in the process of becoming better leaders. The persons who may present the greatest problem are those who think they don't need to learn more about facilitating a group.

Before we take a look at some basic qualities needed for effective small group leadership, it might be helpful to ponder some of the blessings that will come to those who accept the challenge and calling to be a small group facilitator.

**2.** Ask the group to identify possible blessings. As the trainees mention blessings, record them on the chalkboard or on newsprint. A sample list follows.

☛ Getting to know a few people on a more intimate basis

☛ The sense of satisfaction in facilitating an experience of community for people who really long for it

☛ Witnessing the development of a caring community as participants mutually support one another

☛ Thankfulness for the way God's Spirit can open and transform people

☛ Growth in practicing the art of listening, asking questions, and storytelling

**3.** When the list is completed, hand out copies of Training Handout 6, "Helpful Characteristics of Small Group Facilitators." Instruct trainees to complete the exercise found in it.

# The facilitator's job description

**1.** Present the following to the group:

In one sense, a healthy group shares leadership. That is, no one person carries the conversation or the full responsibility for the group process. As a group develops, all the members begin to take ownership and responsibility so that the various needs of participants in the group are being met.

Most groups, however, need a specific leader to initiate the process and oversee administrative details. This person is called a facilitator. Other responsibilities are carried out by the cofacilitator and the host.

Next we will look at qualifications and job descriptions for the small group facilitator, cofacilitator, and host. It is helpful to have a cofacilitator for each group, when possible. Having a cofacilitator is a good way to recruit and train new people to become facilitators when the need arises. The host provides their home or hosts the group in a public place.

**2.** Ask trainees to turn to the "Small Group Leadership Diagram" (Program Resource 7, page 31) and the job descriptions for facilitator, cofacilitator, and host (Program Resources 8, 12, and 13). Review the diagram of a typical small group and job descriptions for the facilitator, cofacilitator, and host.

**3.** Ask if the group would like to add anything. Invite questions and comments.

## Discovering leadership styles

**1.** Present the following to the group:

Everyone uses a mix of leadership styles. Most of us have a style we are most comfortable with and exercise most frequently. It can be helpful to know one's leadership style and both the strengths and weaknesses of our approach.

**2.** Instruct the trainees to turn to Training Handout 7. Review the five basic styles listed.

**3.** Use the discussion questions to allow the trainees to explore their own styles of leadership.

## Review and questions

**1.** Review the outline for this session. Review what has been accomplished. Ask for questions. Some concerns may have to wait for another time.

**2.** Let the trainees know what will be covered in the next session.

**3.** Make any necessary assignments.

Close with prayer. Use "Prayer for the Journey" in Training Handout 1, page 104.

# Session two: Bible study

## Outline:
- Prayer
- Community building exercises
- Biblical reflection
- The priesthood of all believers
- Theological foundations of small groups
- Small groups and traditional Bible study
- One anothering
- The use of multiple choice questions
- Practicing a small group Bible study
- Review and questions

### Materials needed
- General materials: Bibles, pens or pencils, writing paper, chalkboard and chalk or newsprint and markers.
- Training Handouts (one copy of each handout for each trainee): 1, 2, 8, 9, 10A, 10B, 11

### Preparation
- You may want to choose a trainee ahead of time to facilitate the sample Bible study in this session.

## Prayer

Begin with prayer.

## Community building exercises

**1.** Review some of the thoughts about community building from your last session.

**2.** Go around the circle and ask the participants to give their names and the names of those who have given their names before them. If the group knows each other quite well, you can ask the trainees to give not only their name but where they were born or their favorite color or both. This is an exercise in listening.

**3.** Turn to Training Handout 8 (page 112) for additional community building exercises.

## Biblical reflection

**1.** Turn to the Bible passages in Training Handout 2 (page 105) and use one of them for this part of your gathering.

**2.** Take time here for a kind of devotional and inspirational approach to that passage. Ask:

☞ What is God doing or saying to us in this text?

☞ Where do you find yourself in this text?

## The priesthood of all believers

**1.** Present the following to the group:

The priesthood of all believers is a biblical teaching that was recovered in the reformation of the 16th century. The phrase means that each Christian has a priestly or pastoral ministry. Our baptism is, in a sense, our ordination for service to one another and to the world.

**2.** Take time to reflect with the trainees on the following passage in 1 Peter. Think about its application to ministry through small group and how it relates to our pastoral ministry to one another.

In 1 Peter 2:9, we read, "But you are a chosen people, a royal priest-hood, a holy nation, a people belonging to God, that you may declare the praises of him who called you out of darkness into his wonderful light" (NIV).

**3.** Turn to Training Handout 9 (page 113) for an exercise related to the priesthood of all believers.

## Theological foundations of small groups

**1.** Present the following to the group:

We usually operate out of a set of beliefs or values that undergird the ministry we do. While these beliefs are not always articulated or agreed upon, it is helpful to review some of the theological foundations of small groups.

**2.** Distribute Training Handout 10A (page 114). Go over this list with your trainees. You may add others.

**3.** Choose one of the options, litany or confession, to do together.

## Small groups and traditional Bible study

**1.** Present the following information to the trainees:

Most churches that move more intentionally into a small group effort have a history of various adult Bible study programs. These programs have been important and continue to serve a useful purpose. But there is a difference in the way Bible study is used in small groups. It is more relational.

While small groups usually do include some amount of biblical reflection, there is less predictable structure than in most traditional Bible studies. In discipleship groups and support and recovery groups, where participants often study a topic together, there is less didactic instruction and more sharing by participants. Understanding this difference is important lest people become unsettled or feel shortchanged. Small groups are different in these ways:

☞ Relationship-oriented, not content-oriented

☞ Group-owned, not leader-owned

☞ Pastoral ministry, not teaching ministry

In a typical small group session, a portion of the Scriptures is read and studied. God's Word becomes the solid foundation that serves to guide the discussion and keep the group centered on Jesus Christ.

**2.** Distribute and review Training Handout 10B (page 114), "Small Groups and Bible Study."

**3.** Discuss the following questions with your trainees:

☛ How can facilitators assure small group participants that the study of the Bible and learning its content is important even though it may be different from what participants are used to?

☛ A Bible study presented in a lecture format can feel more safe to participants than a discussion-centered Bible study. Why?

☛ How have our culture, our church structure, and our heritage contributed to this?

## One anothering

**1.** Present the following to the groups:

It is amazing to discover the number of times the phrase "one another" is found in the Scriptures. God has always called people to minister to one another.

Small groups, through the work of the Spirit, provide the much-needed support and encouragement that is described in the "one another" passages in the Bible. (For further study on this topic read Richard Meyer's helpful book *One Anothering—Biblical Building Blocks for Small Groups*; see the "References" list for more information.) Training Handout 11 (page 115) lists some of the "one another" passages. The passages form basic building blocks for Christian community.

**2.** Instruct the trainees to find Training Handout 11.

**3.** Assign each trainee a "one another" passage.

**4.** Ask trainees, in turn, to go to the chalkboard or newsprint and write the kind of "one anothering" they find in the Scripture passage. Ask them to turn to the group and finish this sentence:

"In order to _____ one another, I think we must first _____."

Example: "In order to bear one another's burdens, we must first learn to know the person well enough to become familiar with that person's pain and hurts."

If someone has trouble finishing the sentence, let the group complete the sentence together.

**5.** When you have completed the exercise above, turn to the exercise printed in Training Handout 11 and complete it.

# The use of multiple choice questions

**1.** Present the following material on multiple choice questions to the trainees (additional material about asking questions will be covered in Session 3):

Questions serve an important function in small group Bible study. They help to link study materials to the lives of the participants. Small group material uses a variety of types of questions to help the participants interact and share their stories. Some questions are single sentences with no suggested response. Others give the option of multiple answers, allowing the person to choose one or more responses. Both types can be used. Some questions prepare the way for the next question. A person should not feel manipulated by a question.

The advantages of multiple choice questions include:

☛ Multiple choice questions let it be known that there is a range of interpretation of a text. Often there isn't one right answer.

☛ They encourage participants to consider new areas of thought. There often is not time for the group to get much background or think beyond a surface or traditional response, but by giving multiple choice questions you can quickly move beyond the obvious.

☛ They help the shy member and the person who is new to small groups. These people may lack previous knowledge or experience and therefore remain silent unless they are encouraged by some suggested responses.

☛ People usually sense a freedom when given a choice. It always is important to offer the "other" category so if nothing fits, participants can come up with their own response.

☛ They allow a bit of laughter into the discussion by the frequent inclusion of a humorous response with the more serious answers.

☛ Sometimes people don't know how honest to be in responding to a question. If a blunt but honest option is given they may think, "That's where I'm at and I guess I can say it."

**2.** Encourage facilitators to know when and how to mix the types of questions. If there are multiple choice questions, they should be interspersed with open-ended. In the use of multiple choice questions, consider having different members take turns responding to different questions. Not everyone has to answer each question.

**3.** Encourage the trainees to consider how questions are used during the sample small group Bible study that follows. You may want to provide some time for discussing this issue after the group has completed the sample Bible study.

## Practicing a small group Bible study

**1.** Use the sample session from the Bible study in Training Handout 1. (One option for this practice is to ask one of the trainees to lead the others as though it were his or her small group. It is best if you ask the trainee to facilitate the study in advance so that they can prepare.) As the trainer you can either observe or participate.

**2.** Instruct trainees to turn to Training Handout 1, (page 98). Work through the "Discovery" section on Matthew 5:4. Include all of the material through the story of Dorothy.

**3.** When you come to the questions after the William Barclay quote (page 100), break into groups of three or four persons.

**4.** When you have spent approximately twenty minutes on this Bible study, discuss the following questions.

☛ Was the commentary helpful? In what ways?

☛ If you had been a shy person in the group how would you have felt? How would you have been encouraged to participate without feeling pressured?

☛ What is God saying to you in this passage?

☛ In what ways did the Bible study become relational? How did it enable you to relate the text to personal living?

☛ What was not made clear to you? How could this have been improved?

☛ How did the change in group size, from the whole group to groups of three or four, affect your experience of the study? Which group size did you prefer? Why?

## Review and questions

**1.** Review the outline for this session. Review what has been accomplished. Ask for questions. Some concerns may have to wait for another time.

**2.** Let the trainees know what will be covered in the next session.

**3.** Make any necessary assignments.

Close with prayer.

## Session three: mutual support

**Outline:**
- Prayer
- Community building exercises
- Biblical reflection
- Small groups and communication
- Practicing mutual support questions
- The art of storytelling
- The art of listening
- The art of asking questions
- The use of music in small groups
- Review and questions

### Materials needed
- General materials: Bibles, pens or pencils, writing paper, chalkboard and chalk or newsprint and markers.
- Training Handouts (one copy of each for each trainee): 1, 2, 12A, 12B, 13, 14A, 14B

### Preparation
- You might ask a trainee to facilitate the sample Bible study in this session.
- Make an extra copy of Training Handout 12A, (page 116) and cut it apart so that each slip of paper contains one role. Make enough copies for each of the trainees to have one or two roles.
- Review "Small Groups and Communication," page 3.

---

## Prayer

Use the opening prayer of the sample study guide in Training Handout 1. Or you may choose to use a time of silence for participants to connect with God in their own way.

## Community building exercises

In this session you will use gathering questions that relate more to feelings and personal attitudes. Your group has now begun to know each other better and the environment should be more conducive to talking about feelings. Use as much of this as fits your needs and schedule.

**1.** Choose one of these two questions to ask the group.

- ☞ How do you respond when someone lets you know they don't approve of what you have done or said?

- ☞ Tell about a feeling you have had recently that resulted in some action on your part. How did you express your feeling? Did it help?

**2.** Divide into groups of four to discuss for a few minutes the topic "How to improve the singing at the Sunday worship service."

**3.** Before the discussion begins, give each member one or two of the slips of paper you prepared from Training Handout 12A for this session. Not all roles need to be used and some may be repeated.

**4.** Tell only the other members of the group the role they are to play in the discussion.

**5.** Ask them to proceed with discussing the topic and to participate with an emphasis on the role assigned. For example, the trainee assigned the role of doubter will ask questions and make statements that express doubt.

**6.** After five minutes, end the discussion and ask the groups to discuss what role they thought each person was playing. Ask trainees to talk about how the various roles affected the dynamics of the group.

**7.** Hand out the list of roles from Training Handout 12A to the group. Ask them, "What role do you feel most comfortable in?" Discuss for as long as is helpful.

## Biblical reflection

Turn to Training Handout 2 and use one of the Bible passages for this part of your session. Reflections and questions are also located in the handout.

## Small groups and communication

**1.** Introduce the topic of communication by presenting the material "Small Groups and Communication" found in Chapter 8 (page 53).

**2.** Ask the trainees to give examples of how the different points made in that material have been present in the training sessions so far. Encourage specific examples.

**3.** Ask the trainees to list various ways they have experienced positive communication today, or what became difficult for them today because of inadequate communication. What could have improved the difficulties?

**4.** If there is time, play the telephone game, which provides a lighter approach to the topic of communication. Whisper a three-sentence message to the person next to you. Each person in turn passes it to the next person in a whisper (repeating it only once). See how the message changes. Discuss what the game teaches about communication.

## Practicing mutual support questions

**1.** Use this opportunity to allow another trainee to facilitate the discussion. Have the group turn to Training Handout 1 and begin with the "Discovery" section on Exodus 1:22—2:4.

**2.** Suggest that some of the trainees read aloud the options in the first two questions following the Bible passage. Go around the circle for responses. On the second two questions, do not go around the circle; open it up for volunteers to respond. Note for the trainees the difference in participation.

**3.** Allow the group to evaluate both the questions and the way the trainee facilitated the group. Use the questions below to better understand mutual support.

☛ Did anyone share a personal story or experience? How did the group respond? Give an example of how storytelling enabled mutual support to happen.

☛ Did mutual support occur in any nonverbal ways?

☛ When is it good to call for responses from everyone in the group and when is it best to invite volunteer responses? To what does the facilitator need to be sensitive and why?

## The art of storytelling

**1.** Share the following information on storytelling with the trainees. It may be helpful to hand out Training Handout 12B so that trainees can follow the major points of this presentation.

*The Art of Storytelling*

Have contemporary people lost the skill of sharing the stories of their lives with one another? In the past, people sat around the table and talked after the evening meal. Or they drove over to the home of friends or relatives after Sunday dinner and spent the afternoon talking. Some sat on the front porch of their homes and passed the time of day by calling out to neighbors passing by. When do we take the time to share our mundane and important stories? A more important question might be, "Why tell our stories?"

### Why tell our stories?

**Stories define the uniqueness of the person.** As you tell and hear your stories, you learn what and who contributed to making you the person you are today. Therefore, not only do others learn to know you, but you also discover yourself.

**Stories build relationships.** We are created to be in relationship. The Bible urges us to draw near to God, and indicates that God desires to be in relationship with us. We who are created in the image of God also desire fellowship. One of the most effective methods for this relationship to develop is through storytelling.

**Stories can provide inspiration.** When you tell the story of how God helped you survive a terrible loss, it fills others with hope that they, too, can face the losses of their lives. We are inspired by one another's stories rather than by unsolicited advice.

**Stories are one avenue of self-expression.** An important ingredient of good mental health and a sense of well-being is the opportunity for expression. As we tell our stories we express feelings as well as facts. Both are necessary to get the total picture; and both are necessary for true expression.

**Stories connect us with the humanness of others.** While each person is unique, we share many similarities with other humans. In hearing stories of failure and success, sorrow and joy, gifts and losses, we gain perspective and learn to forgive our shortcomings, as well as the imperfections of others.

**Stories pass on values.** While traveling in South Africa, I heard many stories of the sacrifices Black parents made to send their children to school. Through their actions these parents taught their children the value of education. As the stories are told and retold, that value will be passed on to the next generations.

**Stories affirm all people.** Age doesn't matter; neither do sex, race, occupation, intellect or culture. Stories are the great equalizer, for storytelling affirms the contribution of all. Experiences, not an accumulated bank of knowledge, are the focal point.

**Stories develop community.** In Hebrews 10:23-25 we learn about community building. Christians are urged to hold fast the confession of our hope, to stir up one another to love and good works, to meet together, and to encourage one another. Stories are a vital part of confession, stirring up, meeting together, and encouraging.

While storytelling provides all of the above—and more—one of the best reasons for telling stories is that it is so much fun. "Tell me a story," we plead, from the time of early childhood. In adulthood we venture, "Did I every tell you about the time...?" Through all of life we relish storytelling. No wonder it is an important activity in small groups.

## How to draw out another person's story

**A safe place.** The most essential element in freeing a person to share a story—especially one of emotional impact—is the element of safety. When confidentiality and trust are honored, a safe place is available.

**Attitude and body language.** If you are genuinely interested and exhibit warmth and empathy, group members are more likely to feel acceptance. Eye contact, attentiveness, and an unhurried atmosphere contribute to comfort within the group.

**Self-disclosure.** Group facilitators can set the tone for openness by being willing to tell their stories. Don't expect others to do what you yourself are not willing to do. When you share appropriate stories it gives permission to others to do so without them feeling that they are being exposed.

**Questions.** When raising questions within the group, it is helpful if you begin with easy and familiar topics, gradually moving into topics that require more thoughtful and emotional responses. In addition, to assist the group in grasping what the person is saying, use nudging comments and questions to gently probe for further information and details. Examples of nudging comments are: "Would you like to say more about that?" "How did that feel to you?" "Would you care to talk about that?"

**Listen.** This is perhaps the most difficult technique of all. It is such hard work to listen. We prefer to talk or to think about ourselves while others are talking. Instead, we need to focus on the one talking. Someone once said, "Put a muzzle on the muscle in your mouth." That's what most of us struggle to do. People do not feel comfortable sharing their stories if we are not active listeners. It's as simple—and as difficult—as that.

Copyright © Vivian Elaine Johnson. Reprinted by permission.

**2.** Have the trainees divide into groups of three or four. Instruct them to share stories of a proud moment in their life, giving enough background to make the story a way to tell about themselves.

**3.** When everyone has told a story, take a few moments to go over the eight points listed in "The Art of Storytelling" and apply them to each person's story.

**4.** (Optional) While in the same groups of three or four, have trainees tell the story of how their faith has come alive or how you have been spiritually renewed. What were the circumstances?

**5.** Turn to Training Handout 13, "LifeStories/FaithStories," and review some of the questions with the group.

## The art of listening

**1.** To introduce this topic, read the quote in the margin to the group.

**2.** Next read or summarize aloud the following:

Everyone longs to be listened to. When you listen to another, you can give that person a great gift. Small groups provide an excellent atmosphere for genuine listening.

**3.** Ask for a volunteer to sit facing you. Ask this person to listen while you take four to six minutes to tell about a person who has meant a lot to you. Go into some detail as to why that person means so much.

**4.** Then give the volunteer an opportunity to repeat what they heard. Finally, ask the rest of the class to briefly recount and evaluate this listening exercise.

**5.** Have the group divide into pairs. In each pair, one person will listen while the other tells about a person that has been a big influence in his or her life.

**6.** After four or five minutes ask the listener to share what was heard. If time permits they can reverse the roles and do the exercise again. Have the entire group evaluate their experience with these questions about listening:

☞ Did you feel listened to? Why or why not?

☞ What were some of the signals given you that made you feel that the person heard you?

☞ Did the person listening hear feelings that were not necessarily expressed in words?

☞ What verbal sounds or body language gave you the feeling that the person was genuinely listening?

☞ What did you learn from this exercise?

"I know you believe

you understand what

you think I said, but

I'm not sure you

realize that what

you heard is what

I meant."

Julie A. Gorman,
*Community That Is
Christian: A Handbook on
Small Groups*

# The art of asking questions

**1**. Present the following to the group:

Carrying on meaningful conversation is difficult when we do not know anything about the person with whom we are talking. Gaining information helps to establish a bridge between persons who are strangers. Knowing when and how to use effective questioning can be a helpful tool in developing conversational skills. We will focus on how to use open-ended questions. Remember that frequently a person needs to start a conversation with some informational questions. Keep in mind that there are appropriate and inappropriate times and places to ask open-ended questions.

**2**. Distribute Training Handout 14A. Review with the trainees the four types of questions. Use the "Questions to Ponder" for a brief discussion.

**3**. Next, invite the trainees to share with the group two personal interests, especially unusual interests. Ask, "What are two interests you have that really energize you besides your job or your family responsibilities?" Instruct the trainees to only identify their interests, not talk about them.

**4**. As the trainer, you will help the group learn how to ask open-ended questions. Choose one of the interests of one trainee in the group. Instruct the group to brainstorm questions about this person's interest. Encourage them to ask questions that will help them learn more about this interest.

**5**. Write the questions on a chalkboard. Then this person will rank the top three that he or she would like to answer.

**6**. After the person has answered one of the top three questions, the group may ask more questions based on the answer already given.

**7**. Review with the group the list of questions on the chalkboard that were asked of the one person's interest. Place a "C" by those considered closed questions and an "O" by those that were open. (See Training Handout 14A for the definitions of closed and open questions.)

**8**. Ask the group to reword the closed questions to make them more open.

**9**. Continue with the exercises on the art of asking questions in Training Handout 14B.

# The use of music in small groups

**1**. Present the following material to the trainees:

A number of things can be added to small groups that will enhance the experience of community. Music is one of them. Music is a gift of the Spirit that reaches the soul and binds us together in praise of God. It can be used very effectively with little equipment or professional skill.

Small groups do not usually incorporate a worship service into their short time together. Realize your limitations and your primary purpose. However, a time for singing a song or hymn can build community. Music can be used at the beginning or end of sessions.

Some things to think about in planning how to use music are:

- ☛ What songs or hymns do the small group participants know? It is best to use songs that do not require books or written music. Simple songs and hymns from childhood may be good ones to start with.

- ☛ The facilitator doesn't need to be the one to lead the music. See if there is someone who will volunteer.

- ☛ A tape being played for background music can help a group to sing. Also, you may find that a participant plays the guitar, piano, harmonica, or another instrument.

- ☛ Having taped background music while people are gathering can be effective.

- ☛ Use a song or hymn more than once so that people can learn it and sing it without looking at the words.

- ☛ Ask if one of the participants wants to teach the group a song or hymn.

- ☛ Ask if the group has a favorite song or hymn they want to try.

- ☛ If singing doesn't fit your group, don't worry. Don't force it.

**2.** After reviewing these ideas with trainees, try singing with them. Start with something easy. Encourage trainees to discuss how they feel about using music in the small group.

## Review and questions

1. Take time to review the outline for this session. Review what has been accomplished.

2. Ask for questions. Some concerns may have to wait for another time.

3. Let the trainees know what will be covered in the next session.

4. Make any necessary assignments.

Close with prayer.

## Session four: prayer

**Outline:**
- Prayer
- Community building exercises
- Biblical reflection
- Bible study
- Prayer in small groups
- The group covenant and confidences
- Preparing for the first meeting
- Small group details
- Review and questions

### Materials needed
- General materials: Bibles, pens or pencils, writing paper, chalkboard and chalk or newsprint and markers.
- Training Handouts (one copy of each handout for each trainee): 1, 2, 15, 16, 17, 18, 19
- Small group agendas from Part 2 (Program Resources 4, 5, and 6, pages 28-30).

### Preparation
- You might ask trainees to lead the opening prayer and facilitate the sample Bible Study.
- Review "The Small Group Covenant" and "Confidentiality," pages 53-54.

## Prayer

Ask for a volunteer to begin with a brief prayer.

## Community building exercises

**1.** Have the group share a time when they prayed hard for something but it seemed like the prayer was not answered. Ask:

☛ How did it feel?

☛ As you look back on that experience now, what is your understanding of it?

**2.** Ask the trainees to report any personal items or experiences that have developed since your last meeting. What has happened in the world that concerns them?

**3.** You may want to sing a song together.

## Biblical reflection

Turn to Training Handout 2 and use Matthew 26:36-46 for a devotional time.

## Bible study

Turn to the sample Bible study in Training Handout 1. Begin with the Max De Pree quote in "Consider This" and continue through "A Further Look." You may choose to ask a trainee to facilitate this study.

## Prayer in small groups

Communication with God through prayer is central to small group life. However, not everyone participates easily in prayer. Some have had no experience in praying out loud. Children learn to pray more easily than adults. The small group facilitators may not be comfortable with leading prayer. Be sensitive to this. If prayer is not done appropriately in small groups, it can become the reason some will not come to a small group.

**1.** Present the following information:

Prayer is central to our relationship with God. Prayer draws us closer to God and to one another. We don't always understand how it works or how to explain its power. In the Scriptures God calls us to pray for one another (James 5:16). Small groups become a place where participants can pray for others.

These training sessions do not give a thorough study of prayer. Some attention, however, needs to be given to the practice.

When Jesus told Peter that Satan desired to have him that he might sift him like wheat (Luke 22:31-32), he went on to say, "but I have prayed for you that your own faith may not fail." Jesus knew Peter well enough to be specific in his prayers for him. The assurance that Jesus was praying for him no doubt helped Peter in his faith journey. Everyone needs to hear these words from someone who really means it: "I have or I am praying for you."

At the larger worship celebration we join in corporate prayers and general prayers. We pray for groups of people and for people in crisis. We pray prayers of adoration, thanks, and confession. In small groups we are given the opportunity to pray all of these ways, especially prayers for our neighbor's specific needs. In future meetings, we can follow up on the prayers we've prayed. There is something about hearing someone pray to God for us in their own words that binds us together. It tells each of us that we are cared for.

To pray for one another we need to know each other. The mutual support of small groups gives us that opportunity. As trust develops people share things they haven't told others. The small group facilitator and participants become leaders in the prayer life of the church.

**2.** Review with the trainees the information in Training Handout 15 under "Things to keep in mind."

• • • • • • • • • • • • • • • • •

"Therefore confess

your sins to one

another, and pray for

one another, so that

you may be healed."

James 5:16

• • • • • • • • • • • • • • • • •

3. Ask the group to look at "Some methods to use" on the handout and:

   a. Mark a star (★) beside the prayer methods they have participated in,

   b. Put a question mark (?) next to the ones they feel uncomfortable about, and

   c. Mark an exclamation point (!) beside the methods they would be willing to try.

4. Discuss together the following questions:

   ☛ What has been your experience with group prayer, conversational prayer, and praying with others?

   ☛ What apprehensions do you have and what help do you need?

5. Choose one or two new methods of prayer and try them out with the trainees. Afterwards ask, "How did you feel?" Encourage discussion.

## The group covenant and confidences

1. Review the information on the covenant with your trainees. A sample group covenant is in Training Handout 16. (More information on group covenants can be found in Chapter 8 of this section.)

Somewhere near the beginning of a small group it is important to have general agreement on the following:

   ☛ The purpose of the group

   ☛ The shared values

   ☛ The common commitments

   ☛ The arrangement of details

Having a covenant with clearly stated purposes can assist the facilitator in keeping the members on the course they set for themselves.

2. Explain to the trainees that it is helpful to give the general outline of the covenant to small groups during the first session. This provides participants with basic information and will save time.

Covenants, of course, can be discussed and revised at any time. For example, if the small group finds it difficult to start at the agreed upon time, it would be well to renegotiate that.

3. Review the material from Chapter 8 on confidentiality with the trainees. Invite them to ask questions.

4. Encourage the facilitators to find ways to remind the group of the covenant of confidentiality.

   ☛ The covenant might be reviewed periodically.

   ☛ Occasionally an illustration may be used to point out the importance of trust and how intimacy grows out of trust.

   ☛ The group can be asked to pray for openness, trust, and honesty.

# Preparing for the first meeting

**1.** Inform the facilitators that it is now time to think about their first meeting.

**2.** Tell them how the groups will be formed, how many there will be, who will facilitate each group and any other data that is particular to your situation.

**3.** Talk about the importance of preparing for each meeting. Tell trainees that the first meeting will set the pace for group development.

**4.** Deal with fears and questions.

**5.** Review the material on preparing for your first meeting, Training Handout 17, with facilitators and add what is appropriate or lacking.

**6.** Also review the sample small group agendas (see Program Resources 4, 5, and 6, pages 28-30). Note that there is a sample agenda for each of the three types of groups: discipleship, support and recovery, and ministry. Select the agendas most appropriate for your group of trainees, depending upon the type of group they will facilitate.

# Small group details

**1.** Ask the trainees to look at Training Handout 18, "Seating at Small Groups."

**2.** Next, present the following:

In most churches providing child care options is important if you want parents of young children to participate in small groups. The child care issue can silently pose real dilemmas and encourage passive resistance. See the issue from the perspective of parents.

In dealing with the child care issue it will be helpful to:

☛ Remember that you don't want to encourage parents to neglect spending time with their children. Affirm the importance of family time.

☛ Offer options so that participants with children aren't forced into one way to handle it.

☛ Affirm the need for adults to spend time on their own spiritual development and interaction with other adults. They don't need to feel guilty about this.

☛ Let each small group be responsible for the child care needed so that no one person or committee has to solve everyone's request.

☛ Make sure in your promotion that the child care issue is clearly spelled out. Make it very visible and repeat it.

☛ Talk to other churches that have small groups to get new ideas on how to solve the child care issue. Have a pool of ideas to suggest.

☛ Keep in mind that children are important. They are not a problem. They are part of the church. Approach the issue with great compassion for children.

☛ Consider making your group intergenerational where children are welcome and where something is planned for them. Keep in mind that this will significantly change some of the dynamics of the group.

3. Next, review the content relating to social events, Training Handout 19.

4. Allow time for questions.

## Review and questions

1. Affirm and express appreciation to the facilitators for their time and gifts.

2. Review the topics you have covered in this session.

3. Prepare trainees for the next session. If time allows, sing a song together. Close with a prayer and the dismissal blessing:

**Leader:** "Go in peace, serve the Lord."

**Group:** Thanks be to God.

# Session five: ministry tasks

**Note:** If you are training a group of support and recovery group facilitators, use this session last. After Session 4 and before this final session, complete the training session specifically for support and recovery facilitators. See pages 88-94.

## Outline:
- Community building exercise
- Biblical reflection and prayer
- Small groups and ministry tasks
- Small groups and mission
- Welcoming the stranger
- Learning about healthy groups
- How to terminate a group gracefully
- Reports
- The tree of small group leadership
- Claiming the promises
- Closing

### Materials needed
- General materials: Bibles, pens or pencils, writing paper, chalkboard and chalk or newsprint and markers.
- Training Handouts (one copy of each handout for each trainee): 2, 20A, 20B, 21A, 21B, 22, 23A, 23B, 24, 25, 26
- Program Resource 9

### Preparation
- Optional: Find a game that involves cooperation and fun that the group can play as part of the community building exercise.
- Bring enough copies of your church's mission statement and constitution for each trainee.
- Review "Life Cycle of a Small Group," page 55.

## Community building exercise

### Checking in

**1.** If your group has fewer than eight people, have them check in with each other using the questions below. If your group consists of more than eight, first divide into groups of three or four.

☛ What has happened in your life this past week?

☛ What unexpected experience have you had recently?

☛ How have you experienced God's guidance or God's grace in your life this past week?

☛ How do you feel about facilitating a small group?

**2.** Observe how the level of sharing has developed since your first meeting. Ask the trainees what they have seen happening and why.

## Optional game

**1.** If you have decided to do so, play the game you have selected.

**2.** When the game is over, ask the trainees to share what they observed about the group in this exercise.

☞ What happened that contributed to community building?

☞ How does having fun relate to community building?

## Biblical reflection and prayer

**1.** Refer to one of the scriptures in Training Handout 2 and relate it to small group development.

**2.** Let the scripture passages lead you into a prayer that helps to apply the text to daily life.

**3.** Encourage the facilitators to find opportunities to use the scripture passages to guide their prayer time.

## Small groups and ministry tasks

Present the following to the group:

There has been some discussion in previous sessions about the risk of small groups becoming too self-centered. One way to avoid this problem is by focusing on the fourth component of effective groups, the ministry task.

The facilitator needs to always keep in mind the goal of ministry through the small group. At first the primary emphasis is on building community and relational Bible study, but with an eye on ministry. During the early stages of a group's development, encourage participants to choose easier tasks. As time passes, the tasks may become more challenging and involve group activity and participation.

Some ideas that have been used in the beginning stages of a group are found in Training Handout 20A. Review the ideas with trainees. Ask for additional ideas.

## Small groups and mission

Small groups help a church to fulfill its mission to love God and neighbor. As you train facilitators, it is important for the trainees to ponder the question, "What is this church's mission?" If your church has a mission statement, review it with trainees. Your constitution will include a statement of purpose that can also be helpful.

**1.** Pass out copies of your mission statement or important sections in your constitution (or both).

**2.** Ask the trainees to suggest ways in which small groups fit into the mission of your church. Write their suggestions on newsprint. You may want to share the trainees' suggestions with the church board or council.

• • • • • • • • • • • • • • • •

**"If you offer your food to the hungry and satisfy the needs of the afflicted, then your light shall rise in the darkness..."**

Isaiah 58:10

• • • • • • • • • • • • • • • •

## Welcoming the stranger

**1.** Begin by presenting the following material to the trainees (an exercise follows this information):

Small groups are encouraged to welcome new people. The empty or open chair policy is designed to encourage participants to welcome new people into their group. Some groups set up an empty chair at their meetings to remind themselves to invite new people. Small groups can become an important arm of a church's evangelism and outreach.

Persons who may have given up on the church for one reason or another may be open to a smaller gathering where they have the opportunity to share their stories, be cared for, and be heard. Participants may find that neighbors more readily respond to an invitation to a small group meeting than an invitation to a large worship service.

**2.** Review Training Handout 20B for things to keep in mind when thinking about how to welcome new members into the group, especially the unchurched or the persons who are new to the Christian faith.

**3.** After sharing these insights with trainees, divide the group into pairs and ask them to share an experience of either welcoming or failing to welcome a stranger. Have the groups address the following questions:

- ☛ What were the circumstances?

- ☛ What did you do that helped the stranger feel more welcomed?

- ☛ What could you have done?

- ☛ How does this relate to ministry through small groups?

**4.** Have trainees share their suggestions with the entire group.

## Learning about healthy groups

In this part of the session you will deal with a number of issues that relate to the leadership of small groups. Some of them will apply depending on the size and make up of the church and the emphasis being given to small groups.

**1.** Begin by handing out copies of Training Handout 21A, "Signs of a Healthy Small Group." Review the material with the trainees and ask for questions.

**2.** Next, turn to Training Handout 21B, "Things that Choke a Small Group." Again, review the material with the trainees and invite questions. Trainees may want to suggest possible solutions.

**3.** Finally, turn to Training Handout 22, "How to Deal with Monopolizers and Onlookers." Present the material to the trainees and discuss it together. The trainees may want to add their own suggestions to these lists.

## How to terminate a group gracefully

**1.** Keep before the trainees the reality that not all groups make it for the long haul. When it becomes apparent that the group is struggling and may need to terminate, it need not reflect on the facilitator.

**2.** Review Training Handout 23A, "Why Groups Terminate."

**3.** Next turn to Training Handout 23B and review the information about terminating groups with the trainees.

**4.** Ask the trainees if they have any questions about when to terminate a group or if they have had an experience with a group that needed to end. What did they learn?

## Reports

Program Resource 9 (page 33) are examples of report forms that will be helpful in the administration of your groups. You may want to use them as examples or ideas, but feel free to devise your own that will fit your situation.

Review any forms that the facilitators will be asked to use.

## The tree of small group leadership

**1.** Look at the illustration in Training Handout 24. This can be a helpful exercise in allowing the trainees to share their feelings at this point about facilitating a group.

**2.** Give the trainees time to look at the illustration and discuss the question.

**3.** Next hand out Training Handout 25, "Practical Tips for Small Groups." This is a helpful list of reminders that trainees can use to refocus themselves.

## Claiming the promises

Take time to look at Training Handout 26 and go over the promises with the trainees. Ask each trainee to select a verse that they find particularly inspiring and tell why it was chosen.

## Closing

**1.** Make sure that everyone is aware of what the next steps will be.

**2.** Find a way to thank the trainees in a way that is meaningful. A certificate may be in order.

**3.** Ask each person to share what needs they have and how others could pray for them. Then join in prayer for each other.

**4.** Celebrate.

# Support and recovery group facilitator session

**Note:** This training session is designed specifically for facilitators of support and recovery groups and supplements the material in the other training sessions. Offer this session prior to Session 5, "Ministry Tasks."

## Outline:
- Community building
- Prayer
- Why support and recovery groups?
- What is a support and recovery group?
- How can we have a healthy group?
- Unique challenges
- How long should support and recovery groups meet?
- Closing

### Materials needed
- General materials: Bibles, pens or pencils, writing paper, chalkboard and chalk or newsprint and markers.
- Copies of the community resource list (see "Preparation" below), one per person.
- Training Handout (one copy for each trainee): 27.

### Preparation
- Put together a list of organizations and services in the community that can both support facilitators of support and recovery groups and help participants that have special needs which a small group cannot handle. Make the list open-ended so that other community resources can be added by facilitators.

## Community building

**1.** Ask trainees to pair up with another person and answer the following questions:

☛ When you feel discouraged, what person has helped you?

☛ What did he or she do or say that encouraged you the most?

**2.** Have the whole group gather and record their answers to the following question on a chalkboard or newsprint.

☛ What do you see are some of the issues facing your friends and neighbors that could be addressed by a support or recovery group in our church?

Copyright © 1995 Rev. Paul Sorenson. Reprinted by permission.

## Prayer

Offer a prayer that asks for God's guidance as the group seeks ways to minister to others in need.

## Why support and recovery groups?

**1**. Read the following excerpt from *Newsweek:*

> "All of a sudden people are pouring back into churches and synagogues with a fervor that hasn't been seen since the '50s. It appears that a great religious revival is sweeping the land—until you examine the situation a little more closely. Then you'll notice the biggest crowds today often arrive in midweek...
>
> Alcoholics? Third door to the right.
>
> Sex addicts? They meet on Tuesday.
>
> Overweight men who have a problem with compulsive shopping? Pull up a folding chair, buddy. You're in the right place.
>
> Where you are, specifically, is at a support group meeting—one of about 500,000 that will be attended by some 15 million Americans this week." ("Unite and Conquer," February 5, 1990, pages 50-54.)

**2**. Discuss the following question.

☛ Why do you think support and recovery groups are so popular today?

**3**. Present the following information to the group.

Healthy support or recovery groups foster God's hope and healing by conveying the following messages:

**You're not alone.** In our high-tech, increasingly impersonal world, we can feel isolated. In the midst of our pain we can feel all alone. Support groups at their best convey the message "You're not alone." Other people on the same healing journey provide models and a bond of support. "We are here to walk through this difficult time with you; and more important, God is with you."

**It's OK to feel.** A healthy support or recovery group also provides a safe environment where it is "OK to feel." Emotions of sorrow or anger can be expressed without the concern that one is somehow being judged or devalued.

**You can make it.** As people move through the healing process, the support group also conveys encouragement. Others have made it, and they are here to talk about it. Hearing "You can make it!" from others who have been there can inspire us not to lose heart.

**4**. Ask trainees to pair up and tell about a time of personal need, challenge, or pain, when they were able to talk with someone else who had a similar experience.

## What is a support and recovery group?

**1.** Present the following to the group:

You have been hearing the words "support group" and "recovery group." What are they, and how are they unique?

A **support group** can be defined as a small group gathered around a common area of pain, need, or interest. Groups of this kind might bring together people who have lost a loved one, parents of two-year-olds, victims of abuse, or the unemployed. In every case, the perceived need or interest is strong enough in the person to warrant support.

A **recovery group** focuses on the process of healing from and overcoming an addiction or compulsion. Alcoholics Anonymous and Codependents Anonymous groups are the best known, often using the Twelve Step program for recovering alcoholics, drug addicts, or their loved ones. Groups like Overeaters Anonymous and Gamblers Anonymous help those on a journey toward a stronger spiritual base.

Support and recovery groups share many dynamics in common with other types of small groups. The process of learning and support as a group is common to all small groups. At the same time, these groups focus more specifically on the needs of people rather than a task or a topic of study.

Keep in mind that support and recovery group is not:

☛ A class. Although learning will take place, we are there to facilitate, not teach.

☛ A gripe session. In our frustration and anger lies a temptation to complain about the problems in one's relationships. When we keep the focus on our own growth, healing comes faster.

☛ A therapy group. The group's purpose is to share common struggles by using "I" statements rather than analyzing others in the group. This is not a place for intense confrontation.

☛ A cure-all session. Although a person may be facing a complexity of problems, one group cannot address all of them. For example, healing received from a divorce recovery group may lead one to seek help with issues of parenting. However, the divorce recovery group should not try to deal with parenting issues in any kind of in-depth fashion but focus on the divorce recovery process.

**2.** Take time for questions from the trainees.

## How can we have a healthy group?

**1.** Present the following to the group:

The facilitator of a healthy support and recovery group is:

☛ A facilitator. Your task is to keep the discussion flowing and focused on the issue at hand.

☛ A good listener. Listening communicates care, which is what people need most. When group participants notice that you are actively listening, they will learn to do the same with each other.

☛ Assertive. Be sure to set clear ground rules as a group. Even though you have done this, the sharing in support and recovery groups can easily wander off the topic at hand. As in all groups, some people in their pain or confusion can dominate the conversation. A good facilitator learns how to tactfully bring the discussion back on course for the sake of the entire group.

☛ Familiar with the issue. A facilitator need not be an expert (and it's best if you're not), but you have experienced the particular need being addressed, have studied the topic, or attended similar groups so that you understand the basic issues involved. For example, a facilitator of a grief and loss group will be more effective if she or he grasps the stages of grief that most people follow.

2. Discuss the following question and record the trainees' answers.

☛ From your own experience leading or being in a group, what would consider other qualities of a good facilitator?

## Unique challenges

1. Present the following information to the group about participants' initial fear:

The keys to leading a support or recovery group are very similar to any type of small group. At the same time there are some unique challenges to consider:

☛ Participants' initial fear

☛ Participants' acute pain

☛ The chronically needy

☛ The dominator

☛ The nontalker

2. Discuss:

☛ Why might people be afraid to attend a support group? (*Most people are afraid to attend a support group meeting. Shame, embarrassment, worry about what others will think. Some have been known to sit in their car for an hour, trying to muster up enough courage to come in to the meeting.*)

3. Present the following ways to help overcome participants' **initial fear:**

☛ In the promotion of the group. As you are promoting your group, give great care to explain the group's purpose and format. For example:

"Moms R Us" is an informal gathering of moms with preschoolers who want to learn from each other how to cope with the pressures of parenting. We meet for one hour on Wednesday mornings in Room A. We begin with a brief reading and then open discussion. Each week will focus on a different topic related to parenting small children.

☛ In choosing the group name. In selecting a name for the group, choose a name that is inviting and not intimidating.

☛ In choosing where you meet. Make sure your meeting place is safe and nonthreatening, especially for groups that require anonymity. A place that requires participants to walk through public areas will discourage people from coming.

☛ In your first meeting. Be generous with your affirmation in the first session. Congratulate them for having the courage to come.

☛ In sharing your own story. Begin by sharing your own journey and struggle with the issue at hand. This sets others at ease, reminding them that they are not alone and there is nothing shameful about getting help support from others.

**4.** Present the following regarding **acute pain:**

Certain people have reached such a point of deep or chronic need that the group may not provide the best means of support. If the following behaviors or situations (or both) appear, it is usually best to refer the person for professional help:

☛ Suicidal tendencies: the person makes comments suggesting that he or she is contemplating suicide (for example, "I have no reason to live").

☛ Severe depression: the participant seems very withdrawn or despondent. You observe dramatic mood swings or prolonged weeping beyond what one might expect given the situation.

☛ Abuse: The person makes reference to have been physically or emotionally abused, shows signs of abuse, or alludes to having abused someone else.

If any of these situations arise, you as facilitator can follow up in the following ways:

☛ Visit with the person either after the group meeting or pull the person aside while the group continues. The problem cannot be passed over, and yet it may be more than the person or the group is ready to discuss as a group. You may say something like, "Bob, I'm concerned for you. Could we talk about that further right after the meeting?" This communicates to the person that you care. It also sets the rest of the group members at ease by letting them know that the issues will be addressed soon.

☛ Although your group may have committed to confidentiality in the group (what is said here stays here), these conditions can be life threatening, and getting help is more crucial than maintaining this confidentiality. After you have explored the issue a bit deeper, you can approach it this way:

"I am deeply concerned for you, and I need to talk with someone who can help you better than I can. Will you please go with me to talk with someone?" If that person says "Yes," set up a time right then to meet with a professional. If that person is unwilling, then let them know that for their sake you need to call someone anyway.

**5.** Distribute the community resources list that you have prepared and review it with the whole group.

**6.** Present the following information on another unique challenge, **the chronically needy.**

Certain people find their way to support groups because they feel lonely and are looking for a place to belong. That's OK. However, a few either have little desire to deal with the issue or the issue has become

· · · · · · · · · · · · · · · ·

**"Those who wait for**

**the Lord shall renew**

**their strength."**

Isaiah 40:31

· · · · · · · · · · · · · · · ·

their friend. When they share in the group, the same problem emerges time after time, until you as a facilitator and the entire group grow frustrated. Along with lots of prayer, here are some hints to help:

☛ Meet with them individually and share your observations about this person's ongoing expression of need for such an extended period of time. Explore some goals for personal healing and growth. Express your concern that this group doesn't seem to be helping him or her as you had hoped. Listen for feedback, then explore other avenues for support, such as a professional counselor or lay caregiver (if your church has such a program).

☛ Find someone in the group who will take this person under his or her wing for a period of time for personal ministry. Make certain this caregiver has healthy boundaries so the hurting person's need doesn't consume him or her.

**7.** Present the following information regarding **the dominator:**

It is possible you will have someone in your group who talks more than others. Sometimes you will enjoy their input; occasionally you will run across the individual who seems to take over your group—the one who never stops talking. There is no greater threat to the success of your group than the dominating individual.

The following steps can be used to deal with this person:

☛ On your first group meeting discourage anyone from dominating the group. Say, "Everyone participates, no one dominates."

☛ If someone is dominating, break in nicely and say "That's a great idea. Would anyone else like to add anything?"

☛ Sit at a 90-degree angle from this person, not directly across from him or her. This limits eye contact and diffuses power.

☛ Avoid eye contact altogether.

☛ Do not respond to this person's comments. Your response only encourages him or her to talk more.

☛ If the problem persists, you will have to talk to them after the meeting. Be kind, but let the person know that he or she is preventing others from speaking.

**8.** Present the following information on **the nontalker:**

This personality is not destructive to your group, but he or she may need some encouragement to participate in the discussion. The following ideas might help:

☛ Remember, it is OK for him or her to be silent.

☛ Your job is encouragement, not manipulation.

☛ Feel free (at your discretion) to ask a question directly, like "Jennifer, how do you feel about that?"

☛ Encourage them when they do speak. Even if it's slightly irrelevant, let them go. Affirm them.

☛ Spend a minute or two with them before or after the meeting. If they feel that they are supported, they will be more inclined to contribute.

**9**. Ask facilitators to divide into groups of three or four people and do one of the exercises in Training Handout 27.

## How long should support and recovery groups meet?

**1**. Present these options for meeting schedules. Note that they depend upon the purpose of the group.

☛ A series of meetings with a short break between series. Certain groups require a higher level of trust to foster openness than cannot be achieved if newcomers arrive at every meeting. For this type of group a series of meetings with a short break between each series works well. For example, you could meet for ten weeks with the first three weeks open to invite newcomers and the next seven meetings closed.

☛ Weekly open meetings. Other groups need to be open to newcomers every week, such as groups for those who have lost a loved one or dealing with an addiction. When people are experiencing intense emotional pain, they cannot be expected to wait several weeks to receive the support they need. In groups like these, it is helpful to present a brief oral or written orientation to newcomers each week so they can catch up with the group and feel comfortable.

## Closing

**1**. Review the topics you have covered and summarize the training session.

The key to a healthy support and recovery group is simple—caring. As you express the unconditional acceptance of Jesus Christ, participants will sense God's healing touch and be transformed by God's grace.

**2**. Express your thanks to the facilitators.

**3**. Review next steps and take time for final questions.

Close with prayer.

# Ongoing facilitator training

A possible agenda for the regular meeting of the facilitators might be:

## Biblical reflection

Reading and discussion of Scripture that relates to the reason why your church has small groups (see Training Handout 2 for a list of appropriate passages).

## Skill training

Take up one of the topics in the initial training sessions, perhaps one that you didn't use, and expand on it. Training Handout 28 (page 133) lists additional topics that you could ask facilitators to review and select.

An example of the type of material you might use can be found in Training Handouts 29 and 30 (pages 134-135). Handout 29 offers further information on listening skills and Handout 30 provides an exercise on listening.

## Mutual support

Share stories. Break into groups of three or four and have the trainees share with each other their experiences in their small groups. Provide questions to guide their discussion such as:

- ☞ What has surprised you about your group?

- ☞ What has been the most difficult aspect of leading a group so far?

- ☞ What kind of person or dynamic in your group has presented a challenge or opportunity?

- ☞ How have you included prayer in your group?

- ☞ What ministry tasks have you included?

- ☞ What has been the response to each of these?

- ☞ How would you evaluate the material used?

Renew the vision for your small group emphasis.

This involves giving the facilitators another look at the reason why small groups are so vital to the life and growth of the church. This can be done by:

- ☞ Having some members tell how small groups have changed their relationships and sense of belonging

- ☞ Discussing how small groups relate to the mission of the church

- ☞ Addressing any problems or criticisms that have come up in regard to small groups

## Pray together

If the facilitators gather in small groups in follow-up training there can be personal prayers for each other. If they gather together as one group you can use a variety of ways to include prayer. See suggestions in Session 4.

## Sing a song together

Use one that has been used in groups.

## Announcements and refreshments

Review and collect report forms. Look ahead to future meeting dates. Arrange for someone in the group to plan refreshments.

# Training Handouts

# Becoming Wounded Healers

## Focus

**To remember that dark times of grief and pain can be teachable moments and pathways to blessings, and that we can learn from Jesus how to be sensitive to the suffering of others.**

## Community building

Choose from the following as time permits and as members feel comfortable sharing.

### Option
**Take three to five minutes to walk through the immediate area of your meeting place, or just outside if weather permits, to observe an object, happening, or symbol that suggests disharmony or pain. Tell the group about it.**

■ As you go around the circle giving your name, tell how you got your name and how you feel about it. Do you have, or have you had, any nicknames?

■ Choose one of these three and share your answer with the group:

a. Tell about a time when your feelings were hurt, when you felt let down, or were treated unfairly. What helped you through it?

b. Tell about a time you broke up with a boyfriend or girlfriend. What helped you through it?

c. Tell about a time when you experienced grief or pain over the suffering of someone else (a person or group of people).

■ Have people report activity on their assignments from your last session. Review briefly what is remembered from chapter 1.

### Opening prayer
**We are grateful, God, for another day to live, to love, and to be loved. Open us to both the pain and joy that come from following Jesus. Amen.**

Permission is granted for congregations to reproduce this page provided copies are for local use only and the following copyright notice appears: From *Following Jesus: Encouragement from the Beatitudes for a Troubled World* (Intersections Small Group Series), copyright © 1995 Augsburg Fortress

## Matthew 5:4

4 **"Blessed are those who mourn, for they will be comforted."**

### Suffering and compassion

Among other things, Jesus is referred to as a "man of sorrow" and "acquainted with grief." His teachings often included a dimension of life that embraced the redemptive power in suffering. While he did not encourage people to pursue pain or glorify sorrow, he did demonstrate and teach that to be compassionate is to enter into the suffering of others. To mourn may not always mean to weep tears, but it does mean to be deeply concerned to the point of action.

"Blessed are you who weep now, for you will laugh," is the parallel verse from Luke 6:21. It is combined with its opposing woe: "Woe to you who are laughing now, for you will mourn and weep" (Luke 6:25). Both Matthew and Luke remind us that we not only mourn our shared brokenness (sin), we also are called to share in the sorrow and agony of those who suffer at the hands of a sinful society or system.

Following Jesus teaches us to embrace the dark moments of life rather than deny them or make excuses for them. Darkness can include any experience of grief or pain that accompanies our relationships. We accept and address darkness when we take time to listen and be present to each other in our struggles. Such an embrace gives birth to newness and blessing.

■ Share about a time when you saw one of your parents, another family member, or a close friend grieving. What were the circumstances? How did it affect you?

**Discuss as a group.**

■ What things do you think Jesus was talking about when he said, "Blessed are those who mourn"? What are we to mourn?

a. Our own broken relationships, our sins.

**Choose one or two and explain.**

b. The suffering we experience when we become ill or face a personal crisis.

c. The suffering we experience when we are unjustly treated.

d. The suffering of family and friends that causes sorrow in us.

e. Universal suffering through such things as poverty, religious wars, or natural disasters.

f. The pain of an addiction.

g. Other.

■ Which of the above would be the cause of most mourning in our society today? In the church? In you?

**TRAINING HANDOUT 1**

Permission is granted for congregations to reproduce this page provided copies are for local use only and the following copyright notice appears: From *Following Jesus: Encouragement from the Beatitudes for a Troubled World* (Intersections Small Group Series), copyright © 1995 Augsburg Fortress

## Consider this

**"When things go well it is possible to live for years on the surface of things; but when sorrow comes, a person is driven to the deeper things of life."**

—William Barclay

■ Have you ever experienced what Barclay is talking about? Explain.

■ In his book *The Wounded Healer*, Henri Nouwen reminded us that we are not always able to eliminate the pain of others. We are called to share their pain and darkness in such a way that new hope is experienced. How do we do this?

**Choose one and share an example of how it was true for you or someone you know.**

a. Not having words to say but just being present.

b. Willingness to learn about the root causes of the hurt.

c. Being open to face to face encounters with people struggling for personal survival.

d. Finding someone who has been where I am, who understands.

e. Asking the hard questions with compassion.

f. Being honest enough to recognize limitations, failure, and pain.

g. Being comfortable with tears.

h. Other.

■ Jesus became a servant, obedient to God unto death. He was tempted on all points like we are, but without sin. He was misunderstood, rejected, and falsely accused. Jesus was a wounded healer. How does knowing this help us? How did Jesus embrace darkness?

■ In which of the following situations do you think you would be most helpful by entering into the pain of another or sharing in the experience of darkness? Why?

a. The wound of loneliness.

b. Some form of addiction.

c. Having lost touch with God.

d. Unemployment/career crisis.

e. Doubts about religion/God/church.

f. Loss of a loved one.

g. Terminal illness.

h. Poverty/hunger.

i. Wound of rejection.

j. Childlessness.

k. Others.

■ Think of ways that "mourning" has been encouraged where you have worshiped or in your community. Share them with the group.

Permission is granted for congregations to reproduce this page provided copies are for local use only and the following copyright notice appears: From *Following Jesus: Encouragement from the Beatitudes for a Troubled World* (Intersections Small Group Series), copyright © 1995 Augsburg Fortress

TRAINING HANDOUT 1

## Consider this

. . . Dorothy was a perpetual member of the third grade church school class. Every child in the church knew that, when you arrived at the third grade in . . . Sunday School, Dorothy would be in your class. She had even been in the class when some . . . parents were in the third grade. Dorothy was in charge of handing out pencils, checking names in the roll book, and taking up the pencils. . . . It was much later . . . that the world told us that Dorothy was someone with Down syndrome. . . . When Dorothy died, in her early fifties — a spectacularly long life for someone with Down syndrome — the whole church turned out for her funeral. No one mentioned that Dorothy was retarded or afflicted. Many testified to how fortunate they had been to know her.

From *Resident Aliens* by Stanley Hauerwas and William H. Willimon.
(Nashville: Abingdon Press, 1989), 93.

■ What in this story touches you in a special way?

■ How was Dorothy a wounded healer?

■ Can you think of situations where adversity became an opportunity to

# Discovery

## Exodus 1:22—2:4

**22 Then Pharaoh commanded all his people, "Every boy that is born to the Hebrews you shall throw into the Nile, but you shall let every girl live."**

**1 Now a man from the house of Levi went and married a Levite woman. 2 The woman conceived and bore a son; and when she saw that he was a fine baby, she hid him three months. 3 When she could hide him no longer she got a papyrus basket for him, and plastered it with bitumen and pitch; she put the child in it and placed it among the reeds on the bank of the river. 4 His sister stood at a distance, to see what would happen to him.**

■ If you had been an Egyptian when Pharaoh commanded that the Hebrew male babies be thrown in the Nile River, how do you think you would have responded?

a. I'm glad I'm not Hebrew. Those poor people.

b. The government must know something I don't know.

c. I love my country, right or wrong. Love it or leave it.

d. Let's move away so we don't have to get involved.

e. When is the next protest rally? I'm going.

f. I'm going to pray for a change of heart for Pharaoh.

g. I want to meet Hebrews and share their pain.

h. Other.

Remember, if this study theme is used for more than one small group session, introduce subsequent sessions with a "Community Builder" and "Opening Prayer" and end with "Wrap-up."

Discuss as a group.

**TRAINING HANDOUT 1**

Permission is granted for congregations to reproduce this page provided copies are for local use only and the following copyright notice appears: From *Following Jesus: Encouragement from the Beatitudes for a Troubled World* (Intersections Small Group Series), copyright © 1995 Augsburg Fortress

If you had been Moses' mother and found yourself pregnant at that time, which of the following reactions would you have had?

a. Blame God.
b. Self-pity.
c. Anger at Pharaoh.
d. Seeking other's support.
e. Others are suffering too.
f. Resigned to fate.
g. Want to make a basket.
h. Pray for a miracle.
i. Weep with despair.
j. Other.

From your own experience, what are some things to avoid in trying to be helpful to people who are going through dark times?

**Explore and relate.**

Where do you see "basket making" (Exodus 2:3) in the community or nation where you live? That is, where are the signs of hopefulness or stories of people taking action rather than complaining or giving up?

## Consider this

**Leaders (and followers) need to learn not to inflict pain, but to bear pain. . . . If you're bearing pain properly . . . you ought to have the mark of struggle. One ought to have bruised shins and skinned knees.**

From *Leadership Jazz* by Max De Pree (New York: Doubleday, 1992), 139.

What are some of the marks of struggle you carry? What are some skinned knees you see in a church you are familiar with or a member of?

TRAINING HANDOUT 1

## A further look

Read Romans 12:9-15.

**Read text aloud and answer as a group.**

How do Paul's exhortations help us "Rejoice with those who rejoice, weep with those who weep" (12:15)?

Share a time when another person's affection, honor, zeal, patience, prayers, generosity, and/or hospitality made a difference in your life.

Permission is granted for congregations to reproduce this page provided copies are for local use only and the following copyright notice appears: From *Following Jesus: Encouragement from the Beatitudes for a Troubled World* (Intersections Small Group Series), copyright © 1995 Augsburg Fortress

## Discovery

### Matthew 5:10-12

10 "Blessed are those who are persecuted for righteousness' sake, for theirs is the kingdom of heaven.
11 "Blessed are you when people revile you and persecute you and utter all kinds of evil against you falsely on my account. 12Rejoice and be glad, for your reward is great in heaven, for in the same way they persecuted the prophets who were before you."

*Discuss as a group.*

In the first chapter of Exodus we learn that a new king came to power in Egypt who did not know Joseph. Joseph's people, the Hebrews, were growing in numbers and influence. The new king instilled a fear that the Hebrews might leave Egypt. It resulted in a form of genocide, the killing of newborn males.

■ Why do you think Pharaoh took such severe action against the Hebrews?

*Explore and relate.*

■ Do those same elements invite domination and violence today? Explain.

■ Who stood to gain and who stood to lose in the story of fear, violence, and death surrounding Moses' birth and the eventual call for liberation (see Exodus 3:7-8)?

■ Watch for signs of mourning in the news you read or hear in the coming week. Where do you feel the nudge to help, the desire to get more involved? Come ready to share your thoughts at the next session.

■ The Eighth Beatitude reminds us that following Jesus puts us on a collision course with oppressive regimes, institutions, and laws as well as our own greed and tendency toward violence. How have you experienced this opposition? Which side have you been on?

### Consider this

**"I think I have received a new understanding of the meaning of suffering. I came away more convinced than ever before that unearned suffering is redemptive."**

—Martin Luther King, Jr., as he emerged from one of his early prison experiences.

**"Everything I've ever learned well, I've learned from pain . . . and no pain is more poignant and deafening than the pain that comes in relationships."**

From *I Asked for Intimacy* by Renita J. Weems (San Diego: LuraMedia, 1993), 61.

*Respond to these two quotes in light of your study of "Becoming Wounded Healers."*

TRAINING HANDOUT 1

## A further look

Read 2 Corinthians 4:7-12.

■ How can the experience described by Paul be an encouragement to your own life as a wounded healer?

■ When have you felt afflicted but not crushed?

Permission is granted for congregations to reproduce this page provided copies are for local use only and the following copyright notice appears: From *Following Jesus: Encouragement from the Beatitudes for a Troubled World* (Intersections Small Group Series), copyright © 1995 Augsburg Fortress

## Wrap-up

See page 10 in the introduction for a description of "Wrap-up."

Before you go, take time for the following:

■ **Group ministry task**

Ongoing prayer requests can be listed on page 61. See page 62 for suggested closing prayers.

■ **Review**

■ **Personal concerns and prayer concerns**

■ **Closing prayers**

## Daily walk

### Bible readings

**Day 1**   Isaiah 61:1-4
*Called to comfort all who mourn.*

**Day 2**   Luke 19:41-44
*Jesus weeps over Jerusalem.*

**Day 3**   Isaiah 53:1-3
*He was a man of sorrow.*

**Day 4**   Psalm 30:4-5
*Joy comes in the morning.*

**Day 5**   1 Cor. 12:24b-26
*One suffers, all suffer.*

**Day 6**   Jer. 31:15-17
*Rachael weeps for her children.*

**Day 7**   John 11:28-37
*Jesus weeps at death of Lazarus.*

### Thought for the journey

To minister to others calls for a recognition of the suffering of one's own heart, which makes our wounds available as a source of healing.

### Prayer for the journey

God, help us to enter more fully into our own grief as well as the pain and sorrow of others so that we might experience new hope and courage to go forward through your Son, Jesus Christ. Amen.

### Verse for the journey

"Weeping may linger for the night, but joy comes in the morning" (Psalm 30:5).

Permission is granted for congregations to reproduce this page provided copies are for local use only and the following copyright notice appears: From *Following Jesus: Encouragement from the Beatitudes for a Troubled World* (Intersections Small Group Series), copyright © 1995 Augsburg Fortress

TRAINING HANDOUT 1

# Biblical affirmations for small groups

The idea of God working through small gatherings of followers can be found throughout the Scriptures. The following passages are just a few examples. Watch for other connected passages as you read your Bible. Faithful reading of God's word calls for careful observation, creative imagination, and receptivity to what God is actively saying to us in a particular passage.

## Acts 2:41-47

### Observe and Imagine

■ The new disciples devoted themselves to four things, one of which was *koinonia*, meaning *fellowship* or *community*.

■ All who believed were together and held things in common. Everyone's need was met. People looked out for each other. To do this they had to know each other. That takes time and effort.

■ They spent time together both in the temple and in homes. Both corporate worship and small group gatherings were practiced. There was a need and a hunger for both.

■ The people practiced generosity. They shared their lives with each other. Their religion was not a private affair.

■ Growth was the result. New people were added to the church. People's lives were changed. People are attracted to places where there is genuine love.

## Acts 5:42 and Acts 20:20

### Observe and Imagine

■ Both the original apostles and Paul met with people in home gatherings as well as the larger gatherings in the Temple.

■ They did not disconnect or abandon their allegiance to the Temple. They stayed connected to the larger expression of the body of Christ, the church—no church-hopping or quitting.

■ The house church was a common practice in the early church. It was one way each person felt involved and cared for through smaller gatherings.

## 1 Corinthians 12:12-26.

### Observe and Imagine

■ Paul is helping the church in Corinth work through some of their problems, one of which was a divisive spirit and the feeling that some were better Christians than others. Faults were not hidden.

■ We all have something in common. We drink of one Spirit. We all have received grace. We are baptized into one body. We all belong to Jesus and, therefore, have a connection to one another.

■ As different members of the body, we discover that we need each other. Only as we relate to each other are we able to stay alive and is the body able to function as a whole.

■ The members of the body need to care for one another. If one suffers, all suffer. We need to be in touch with each other if we are to know when one suffers.

## Luke 8:1-3, Mark 15:40-41, and Luke 23:55—24:12

### Observe and Imagine

■ The community that followed Jesus included men and women.

■ The formation of a mixed community of men and women took courage. In those days the mixing of genders was not looked upon with favor.

■ Joanna was married. Her husband is named (Luke 8:3). This suggests her managing two careers, wife/mother and disciple/ministry. It can be done. Jesus didn't forbid it.

■ At the cross and the Easter tomb the women were still together. They supported each other. They ministered together. They had not given up hope or fled. Maybe they could not have done it without the support of a small group.

TRAINING HANDOUT 2

# Biblical affirmations for small groups

■ Women testified to men. They were the bearers of good news. Even those we sometimes think are not qualified can be the very ones that God uses to bless us.

## Luke 15:1-2

### Observe and Imagine

■ Jesus did not hesitate to be with people who were outcasts. Their past, reputation, social status, or observance of the law were not criteria for being in the company of Jesus.

■ Tax collectors and other outcasts were attracted to Jesus. Perhaps this was because they felt accepted and welcomed. Where do people find such inclusiveness today?

■ That Jesus ate with them suggests a level of intimacy. Eating together was a sign of bonding, closeness and trust.

■ Some of Jesus' small group experiences were not looked upon with favor. People complained and criticized. He broke with tradition. He was willing to risk facing opposition. It must have hurt him.

## Exodus 18:13-27

### Observe and Imagine

■ Moses, the leader of Israel in the wilderness, had a problem. He was doing too much by himself. He was getting burned out.

■ People let him do too much. Why didn't those close to him say something? Where was his support group?

■ Leaders sometimes think they are alone or that they have to be in control of everything. Moses perhaps thought he was doing God's will. He needed honest confrontation from someone he trusted.

■ Jethro's suggested administrative strategy made sense, it worked, it called for lay leadership and an opportunity for everyone to l be cared for.

■ A unit of ten seems workable. People can learn to know and love ten people with some integrity, but not one hundred or one thousand.

## Hebrews 10:23-25

### Observe and Imagine

■ The setting is a church in danger of letting go, giving up hope, turning back. Discouragement and doubt were rampant.

■ Suggestions and reminders are given to help them rekindle the fire within.

■ We are called to minister to one another, lest we lose what has begun in our lives.

■ One secret is not to neglect to meet together, even though some argue that it's not that important.

■ Encouraging one another is our ministry.

■ We only have today. To procrastinate is dangerous.

## Matthew 26:36-46

### Observe and Imagine

■ Jesus wanted to be with his disciples during a difficult time. He took them to Gethsemane. He did not go alone.

■ Jesus wanted a small intimate group to support him, so he took Peter, James, and John. The four of them made a small group. Some things we only reveal to a small group.

■ Jesus could be honest about his feelings to a small group. He said he was deeply grieved. It took a trust level for this to happen.

■ Jesus came back to be with the twelve and found them sleeping. He did not hesitate to let them know of his disappointment. Jesus was honest. In that moment he needed group support.

■ In times of heaviness and stress, we feel the need to pray. It is good to know that others are praying with us and for us.

TRAINING HANDOUT 2

*Starting Small Groups—and Keeping them Going.* Copyright © 1995 Augsburg Fortress. May be reproduced for local use.

# Benefits of small groups

Small groups support and supplement the church's total ministry. Consider the following benefits:

■ **Lay people do the pastoring.**
Group participants minister to one another. Spiritual lives are nurtured and challenged to grow by personal attention and accountability in the group, facilitated by a trained lay leader. Special needs are given immediate and personal attention and prayer. Small group facilitators assist the ordained pastor and other paid staff by extending care to more church members. Because small group facilitators serve an important function, it is imperative that they be well trained and cared for continually.

■ **Small groups offer mutual support.**
Small groups provide a safe, inviting environment for participants to tell the stories of their life journey. Group participants learn to share honestly with a trusted few. They receive support and grow.

■ **Participants' lives are changed.**
Small groups have proven to be fertile ground to produce changed lives. Participants hear and tell stories of faith. Participants find courage to make changes in their own lives after hearing the stories of God's work in others' lives.

■ **Long-term commitments build trust.**
While there is value in short term involvement in church programs, small groups are suited toward building lasting relationships with the group. A twelve month commitment, for example, allows for a level of trust, honesty, and openness that is needed for growth. Small groups take us beyond the casual relationships we have at the fellowship hour on Sunday.

■ **Ministry happens with accountability.**
Many church members don't get involved in ministry through the church because of a volunteer system of recruitment. Other members use so much energy dealing with the hurts and pain of life that no energy is left to help others or get involved in the wider ministry. Small groups provide a personal accountability component that enables more people to be responsible for ministry. When their pain is shared or healed they are ready to listen to the hurts in the community around them.

**TRAINING HANDOUT 3**

# Working definitions of small groups

"A Christian small group is an intentional, face to face gathering of three to twelve people on a regular time schedule with a common purpose of discovering and growing in the possibilities of the abundant life in Christ."

Roberta Hestenes,
"Building Christian Community
through Small Groups,"
page 27.

"A community group is a group of eight to fifteen people who get together in homes to build friendships, enjoy light, relational discussion of Scripture, and develop a network of care and support among each other."

Nick Taylor
Coastland Community Church
Irvine, Calif.

"A small group is a regularly scheduled gathering of three to twelve people (not more), whose chief purpose is to experience Christian community through honest, personal conversation, through study (not lecture) that is relevant to daily living, through genuine caring and support for one another, and through discovering the meaning of compassion by practicing ministry and prayer."

George S. Johnson

Training Handout 4

*Starting Small Groups—and Keeping them Going.* Copyright © 1995 Augsburg Fortress. May be reproduced for local use.

# Four essential components in small groups

**Prayer:** growing closer to God and to each other by praying for each other in a variety of ways.

**Biblical reflection:** receiving God's word. Looking at a biblical text with the goal of relating it to one's daily journey of faith.

**Mutual support:** learning to listen to each other. Sharing stories and care, discovering the value of building community.

**Group ministry task:** blessed to be a blessing.  A group learns accountability as participants take on specific tasks to serve their church or the wider community.

Training Handout 5

# Helpful characteristics of small group facilitators

Following is a list of characteristics that are helpful for facilitating small groups. No one person is good at all of them.

1. Choose the four or five you feel the most positive about in yourself. Place an A by them.

2. Then choose four or five where you need some improvement. Place a B by them.

3. Share your lists with three or four others.

____ Friendly

____ Willing to express feelings

____ Positive attitude

____ Enthusiastic

____ Withholds judgment

____ Remembers names

____ Sensitive

____ Perseverance

____ Encourager

____ Smiles

____ Good listener

____ Approachable

____ Organizer

____ Caring

____ Follows through

____ Teachable

____ Enjoys people

____ Growing relationship with Christ

____ Attends worship regularly

____ Can keep a confidence

____ Good sense of humor

____ Able to say "I don't know"

____ Able to handle conflict

____ Affirming

____ Not needing to be in control

____ Able to clarify things

____ Patience

____ Desire to serve

____ Able to steer discussion

____ Gives God the credit for growth and successes

Training Handout 6

*Starting Small Groups—and Keeping them Going.* Copyright © 1995 Augsburg Fortress. May be reproduced for local use.

# Five basic styles of leadership

### 1. Helper

- Enjoys being a team player
- Works well behind the scenes
- Good motivator and encourager
- Careful not to take stands on controversial issues or to control people

### 2. Mover

- Wants to get things moving
- Makes decisions easily
- Dislikes committees
- Self-starter and not afraid of failure

### 3. Unifier

- Sees the good in each person, uncovers others' potential
- Works at consensus and unity
- Avoids controversial issues or situations
- Verbally affirms and makes people feel like they are important

### 4. Organizer

- Thinks things through carefully, analyzes
- Asks questions that get beneath the surface
- Cautious about risk taking and change
- Wants things well planned and organized

### 5. Feeler

- Open to feelings and expressions of feelings
- Good listener, able to read between the lines
- Patient, works through conflict or tension
- Doesn't always follow the agenda or the lesson

## Discussion questions

1. Which of these styles best describes how you think you come across in a group? What would be number two?

2. Which one do you need to work on in order to help a group develop?

*Starting Small Groups—and Keeping them Going.* Copyright © 1995 Augsburg Fortress. May be reproduced for local use.

Training Handout 7

# Community building exercise

■ Divide into groups of three or four.

■ Take a few minutes to fill in the proper responses. Circle your choices.

■ Share your response with the others in your smaller group.

1. When I go out to eat I often order:
   - a. Fish
   - b. Hamburger
   - c. Red meat
   - d. Chicken
   - e. Salad or soup
   - f. Something plus dessert
   - g. Pizza
   - h. Depends on who's paying

2. When I listen to music on the radio I usually prefer:
   - a. Classical
   - b. Jazz
   - c. Hard rock
   - d. Christian rock
   - e. Country western
   - f. Something romantic
   - g. Band music
   - h. Tunes from great movies

3. If I have a day free from work and family responsibilities, I enjoy:
   - a. Reading a good book
   - b. Doing some sport activity
   - c. Shopping and eating out
   - d. Visiting with a friend
   - e. Going for a walk, then nap
   - f. Seeing a movie with a friend
   - g. Finding a place to be alone
   - h. Catching up on writing or other hobby

Option: Share one of your pet peeves (something that really upsets you) with a small group of three to four people.

Training Handout 8

*Starting Small Groups—and Keeping them Going.* Copyright © 1995 Augsburg Fortress. May be reproduced for local use.

# Pastoral ministry in small groups

What does the priesthood of all believers mean for ministry through small groups? How can we be priests to one another?

Add your thoughts about and applications of the priesthood of all believers to the following:

■ God does not expect our pastor(s) to do all the pastoral ministry among us. Neither should we.

■ Pastoral ministry means caring for the spiritual and physical well being and growth of one another.

■ No follower of Jesus is exempt from pastoral ministry. We are all ministers. Our church has_____(fill in the number) ministers.

■ Baptism is also a kind of ordination service where the baptized are ordained for service in the kingdom of God. At a baptism, we can all renew and remember our ordination to ministry.

■ The church will be stronger and more effective when everyone realizes that they have a priestly function.

■ The idea of a priesthood of all believers suggests that many responsibilities, previously delegated solely to the ordained pastor, be shared by all Christians.

■ Our pastoral ministry as lay people is more likely to happen in small groups where we learn to know a few people on a more intimate level.

■ The Holy Spirit works through the priesthood of all believers to revive the experience of community in our churches and empower us for ministry.

■ As a priest, I am commissioned by God to listen to my sisters and brothers as they share their hurt, their sins, their struggles. I am also called by God to assure them of God's forgiveness, God's love and God's presence.

■ Small groups can be a place where the absolution is experienced, though not pronounced in liturgical language.

■ Prayer for one another is a priestly function that takes on personal meaning in small groups.

■ The priesthood of all believers does not take away the need for, or the role of, an ordained ministry.

■ Our pastors help to equip us through word and sacrament for our priestly ministry.

*Starting Small Groups—and Keeping them Going.* Copyright © 1995 Augsburg Fortress. May be reproduced for local use.

**Training Handout 9**

# A: Theological foundations of small groups

■ We are created in the image of God whose nature is communal.

■ God created us male and female.

■ We are created as social beings, meant to live in community.

■ Our potential is best realized in a supportive community.

■ God related to people through a covenant community before the time of Christ.

■ Small groups challenge the sins of alienation, estrangement and separation.

■ Our common bond is forgiveness and faith in Jesus, not our sameness or our achievements.

■ We are called to witness; to share our stories of God working in our lives.

■ We belong to the priesthood of all believers. We all are called to pastoral ministry.

■ We change and are transformed as we live in community, accountable to one another.

■ We are all important in the family of God.

■ Jesus provided an example for us when he ministered to small groups.

■ The kingdom of God is more about relationships than doctrines or rituals.

■ Spiritual gifts are often best discovered and affirmed in small gatherings.

Make this a group exercise by using this as a litany or a confession of faith. For a litany, the response after each sentence can be "Teach us to more fully understand and appreciate" or "For this we offer our thanks and praise."

As a confession of faith, begin each statement with "We believe that..."

# B: Small groups and Bible study

Small groups will differ from some people's experience in Bible study, because in small groups:

■ A primary purpose is fellowship, caring, and support, not to learn everything one can about a given passage or book, although that can happen as well.

■ Questions raised about a passage are personal, practical, and relevant to current living, rather than theoretical.

■ Answers to questions and insights come from participants in the group rather than a teacher.

■ Usually no preparation is expected from participants.

■ Time is spent on insights of a personal nature as well as on the content of a text. Probing the depths of a passage and academic questions generally are not a priority.

■ The study of the Scriptures includes facing important personal discipleship issues and learning to love one another as Jesus loved.

■ Knowledge of the Bible is not assumed. Those who know the Bible well and those don't can participate equally.

■ Living with unanswered questions about a Bible passage is acceptable.

■ Members are encouraged to ask, "What does the Bible say about the kind of people we need to be?" and "What are we doing about it?"

■ Opportunities for members of a small group to tell their faith stories as they relate to the Bible are intentional. In most traditional Bible studies there is not time for this.

Training Handout 10

*Starting Small Groups—and Keeping them Going.* Copyright © 1995 Augsburg Fortress. May be reproduced for local use.

# One anothering

■ "This is my commandment, that you love one another as I have loved you" (John 15:12).

■ "With all humility and gentleness, with patience, bearing with one another in love, making every effort to maintain the unity of the Spirit in the bond of peace" (Ephesians 4:2-3).

■ "And be kind to one another, tenderhearted, forgiving one another as God in Christ has forgiven you" (Ephesians 4:32).

■ "But if we walk in the light as he himself is in the light, we have fellowship with one another, and the blood of Jesus his Son cleanses us from all sin" (1 John 1:7).

■ "Bear one another's burdens, and in this way you will fulfill the law of Christ" (Galatians 6:2).

■ "Therefore encourage one another and build up each other, as indeed you are doing" (1 Thessalonians 5:11).

■ "Be subject to one another out of reverence for Christ" (Ephesians 5:21).

■ "Therefore confess your sins to one another, and pray for one another, so that you may be healed" (James 5:16).

■ "Let the word of Christ dwell in you richly; teach and admonish one another in all wisdom; and with gratitude in your hearts sing psalms, hymns, and spiritual songs to God" (Colossians 3:16).

■ "Love one another with mutual affection; outdo one another in showing honor" (Romans 12:10).

■ "And let us consider how to provoke one another to love and good deeds, not neglecting to meet together, as is the habit of some, but encouraging one another, and all the more as you see the Day approaching" (Hebrews 10:24-25).

■ "That there may be no dissension within the body, but the members may have the same care for one another" (1 Corinthians 12:25).

**Exercise:** Place a number next to each verse which corresponds with how you see yourself in relation to a "one another" ministry.

1 = doing fairly well, on the way

2 = need to improve, lacking

3 = not involved, unfamiliar, need to start

Share an example of each of the numbers you have given for yourself with a group of three or four and explain why you gave yourself that number.

Which of the above one anothering ministries are more likely to happen first in small groups? Why?

**Training Handout 11**

# A: Roles in Groups

**Talker:** one who often speaks up first, has readily available ideas, is not hesitant to talk, and may not listen well to others.

**Reconciler:** one who sees good in everyone's point of view, tries to blend ideas, uses compromise, avoids conflict, and keeps the peace.

**Doubter:** one who has questions about most ideas, needs strong proof before moving forward, and is not willing to risk very much.

**Clarifier:** one who wants to be clear about the issues, clear about the group's goals, and clear about what people are saying.

**Joker:** one who sees humor in most situations, is able to get people to laugh, is sometimes not serious enough, and sometimes uses humor to avoid getting at feelings.

**Feeler:** one who expresses feelings easily, is sensitive to how others might feel, and who reads between the lines to get at feelings.

**Mover:** one who moves the group along towards its goal, brings the group back if they become sidetracked, and is able to summarize and suggest action.

# B: The art of storytelling

## Why tell our stories?

- Stories define the uniqueness of the person.
- Stories build relationships.
- Stories can provide inspiration.
- Stories are one avenue of self-expression.
- Stories connect us with the humanness of others.
- Stories pass on values.
- Stories affirm all people.
- Stories develop community.

## How to draw out another's story

- Create a safe place.
- Show an inviting attitude and body language.
- Tell your story first.
- Ask easy questions first.
- Listen: focus on the one talking.

Copyright © Vivian Elaine Johnson, Reprinted by permission.

*Starting Small Groups—and Keeping them Going.* Copyright © 1995 Augsburg Fortress. May be reproduced for local use.

# LifeStories/FaithStories

The following questions have proven to be helpful in getting people to share their stories without feeling threatened or embarrassed. They can be used as you gather or as you offer mutual support in your small group discussion. It's good to have questions ready to use when the time seems right.

## Sample LifeStories Questions

■ What was one of the most courageous things you ever did?

■ Describe a neighbor who was difficult to live with.

■ Describe an exciting or unusual trip you have taken.

■ Tell about a book or article you read recently.

■ What was one of your foolish purchases? Why?

■ Tell about an incident with a car.

■ Tell about an experience that made you feel close to nature.

■ Tell about a fun game you have played.

■ Describe something unusual about a wedding you've attended.

■ Name someone or something that influenced you in choosing your work.

■ What is one of the first ways you earned money?

■ Describe one of the worst weather conditions you have been in.

■ What is something satisfying about your work?

■ Tell about a time when you slept outdoors.

■ Describe a place you lived while growing up.

■ Tell about a movie that moved you deeply.

## Sample FaithStories Questions

■ What social justice issues concern you? Why?

■ What does your baptism mean to you?

■ What living or historical person would you like to talk to about their faith?

■ How do you answer the question: "Why do some people suffer so much?"

■ What song or piece of music says something about your faith? In what way?

■ What is one of your favorite stories in the Bible? Why?

■ Talk about a person who influenced your faith life.

■ Talk about one of the Ten Commandments that says something important to you.

■ Tell about an experience that almost seemed supernatural to you.

■ Tell about an act of injustice that troubles you.

■ What causes you to be a hopeful person?

■ How has your understanding of the Christian faith changed since you were a child?

■ Describe a crisis that pushed you closer to God.

■ What effect does nature have on your faith?

■ Tell about something you did as a volunteer that your faith motivated you to do.

■ Tell about a time when Jesus seemed especially close to you.

■ What is one thing that could be done to help various races understand and respect one another?

■ Tell about a difficult loss or experience in your life.

■ Identify a belief with which you have struggled. In what way?

These questions are taken from the game *LifeStories: Christian Version*, created by Wilfred Bockelman, Truman Howell, and Vivian Johnson.

Copyright © 1994 Talicore. Reprinted by permission.

*Starting Small Groups—and Keeping them Going.* Copyright © 1995 Augsburg Fortress. May be reproduced for local use.

Training Handout 13

# A: Types of questions

**Closed:** Leads to a one-word answer; does not invite a person to expand. "Do you like to cook?" "How long have you been cooking?"

**Open:** Allows a person to talk about reasons, feelings, history, and so on. "Why do you like to cook?" "What was an unusual experience with food?"

**Informational:** "When did you move to California?"

**Feeling Level:** "How do you feel about living in California?"

Most people tend to ask informational or closed questions. Open questions help others to tell things about themselves they want to tell you.

## Questions to ponder

■ Can you give some additional examples of open questions?

■ How do you feel when friends ask you feeling (open) questions?

■ What should one do when a person does not answer your question but instead gives unsolicited information on another topic?

■ How can you tell when your question has made the other person nervous or uneasy? What should you do?

# B: The art of asking questions

Review the following material and then complete the exercise as a group.

1. Answer questions with questions. Don't "tell" when you can "ask."

Example: "How do you know Christianity is the only right religion?"

**Not:** "Because the Bible says so."

**Better:** "That's a good question. How do we know?"

2. Deal with feelings as well as facts.

**Not:** "How many times have you had a run-in with your boss this last year?"

**Better:** "How do you handle serious conflict with your boss?" "What kinds of feelings do you go through?"

3. Avoid "yes" or "no" questions.

**Not:** "Is it hard to be a parent?"
**Better:** "What is hard about being a parent?"

4. Don't sermonize with your questions.

**Not:** "Why does God not want wives to work outside of the home?"
**Not:** "Why doesn't every Christian tithe like the Bible says we should?"
**Better:** "What do you think about the practice of tithing?

5. Avoid questions with right answers.

**Not:** "What does the Bible say is the only correct way to discipline a child?"
**Better:** "What encouragement do we find in Scripture to help parents who are struggling with discipline issues?"

## Exercise:

Look at the following questions as a group. Especially when dealing with sensitive or controversial subjects, asking questions is an art. Determine which questions effectively encourage conversation and which do not. Note why you made your choices.

1. Why does the Bible say sex is wrong?
2. Who are some Bible characters who had trouble with sex?
3. Have you ever had premarital sex?
4. Don't you think most women provoke rape in one way or another?
5. Do you think Jesus was ever tempted sexually?
6. Why is the church so reluctant to talk about human sexuality?
7. If God understands our sex drive, why did he make us mature so early?
8. How should a Christian handle sexual temptations?

Now choose one or two less effective questions and rewrite them so that they encourage conversation.

*Starting Small Groups—and Keeping them Going.* Copyright © 1995 Augsburg Fortress. May be reproduced for local use.

# Prayer in small groups

## Things to keep in mind

- People are at different places in their prayer life. Some have never prayed aloud in their own words. Avoid rewarding or judging those with more or less experience.

- Prayer is an important component in small groups. Don't neglect it just because it isn't easy to please everyone.

- Think in terms of development. Move gradually forward but expect people to grow. Appreciate progress.

- Ask for the participation of the group regarding the prayer component. Assure them that no one will be embarrassed or forced to participate.

- Prayer develops a consciousness of God's presence.

- Experience is the best teacher. We don't learn to pray by reading a book. We learn to pray by praying.

- Use a variety of ways to encourage prayer. Let the group know that you want it to be a positive experience.

- At some point in your early meetings ask the participants to share their experience with prayer from childhood to the present. Then ask them what experience they have had in praying in a group.

- Let the group know about your own experience in learning how to pray. Be honest about your struggles.

- Suggest that the group take a group picture. Make copies for everyone. Keep it in a visible place as a reminder to pray for each participant in the group.

Training Handout 15

# Prayer in small groups

## Some methods to use

■ **Prayers that are read.** In most small group study guides you will find written prayers. You can also find them from other resources. Call on volunteers to read these prayers or read them in unison. It's a good way to start.

■ **The facilitator prays.** The facilitator can set an example by preparing a prayer and helping others to learn how to do it. Don't use long prayers that intimidate those who are beginners in praying aloud.

■ **Silent prayer.** Set aside two or three minutes for this. You may suggest topics to pray about. Let the participants know how you will end this time of prayer.

■ **Written prayers.** Give people time to write a short prayer on a piece of paper. Then suggest that those who are willing can read it aloud.

■ **Circle prayer.** Sit or stand in a circle. Holding hands can be optional. Invite volunteers to share a brief prayer. Use the silent moments for prayer as well. Assign someone to close with a prayer. Sometimes you can begin by praying the Lord's Prayer in a circle.

■ **Prayer requests.** Ask the participants to share special needs that can be remembered in prayer. They can be personal or communal needs. The participants may prefer to write them on a sheet of paper. Then call for volunteers to take one and say a simple prayer about that request. As a starter you can go around the circle and ask volunteers to share a request. Then tell them that the mention of a request was a prayer. Just say "Amen" and remind them that God heard the request.

■ **Popcorn prayer.** The facilitator begins with a brief prayer such as, "Lord we are thankful for..." and then group participants randomly complete the sentence. No introduction or amen is needed. Words pop up from different places. You can use this with specific topics or as a general prayer.

■ **Designated prayer:** Ask someone in advance to lead an opening or closing prayer. This will give the person time to prepare. The prayer can be read or offered spontaneously.

■ **Sentence prayer:** Often people are helped to pray aloud if given a sentence to complete. Ask them to complete a sentence like:

Lord, I thank you for _____

Lord, forgive me for _____

Lord, help my friend _____

Lord, help me to be more _____

Lord, help me to let go of _____

Lord, give me the courage to _____

Lord, one of my fears I need
help with is _____

■ **Specific prayer:** As the trust level grows and the participants become more comfortable with prayer, you can ask them to share specific concerns or personal needs. Then ask each participant to pray for the one on their left. Let them know this ahead of time so they can listen carefully. This makes prayer personal and specific.

■ **Laying on of hands:** On certain occasions it may be appropriate to ask one or more persons to lay their hands on one participant who needs special prayer. They can place a hand on the head, shoulder, or back. The touch can be affirming.

■ **Praying while singing:** Many hymns and songs have specific prayers in their lyrics. Once in a while suggest that your prayer time include or be the song you sing.

■ **Spontaneous prayer:** When a special need arises and it seems appropriate, take time right then to say a prayer or call for silent prayer. You don't need to wait for the appointed prayer time.

■ **Prayer journal:** Encourage participants to write down prayer requests that are shared in the group. As participants report back, they can check off progress made. Also, encourage participants to jot down feelings or ideas about prayer as they come to them. Include a list of answered prayers.

Training Handout 15

*Starting Small Groups—and Keeping them Going.* Copyright © 1995 Augsburg Fortress. May be reproduced for local use.

# Sample small group covenant

## Group purpose

- To get to know one another and become a caring community.

- To support one another through listening, sharing, praying, and being present to one another.

- To discover meaning in God's word and apply it to our lives.

- To enjoy one another's uniqueness and take responsibility for our own adventure in Christian growth.

- To share ideas about how we can minister together in Jesus' name.

## Group arrangements

We will meet every _____ for _____ sessions.

Our beginning time will be _____ and each session will be approximately _____ hours.

Our meeting place will be _____.

My turn for refreshments will be _____.

Child care and transportation arrangements are:

_____

_____

Our group facilitator is _____

(phone number: _____).

## Group values

- We agree to make our meetings a top priority and attend regularly.

- We will pray for one another.

- We will not give advice to one another, attempt to fix or judge no matter what is shared, unless we are asked first.

- We will keep personal things spoken in this group within this circle, in order to provide the atmosphere of openness and trust.

- We will strive to become a caring community by sharing our experiences, our struggles, our feelings, our joys, our hurts, and our questions, as we may freely decide to do.

- We will welcome new members into our group.

## Group participants

| Name | Phone Numbers |
|------|---------------|
| _____ | _____ |
| _____ | _____ |
| _____ | _____ |
| _____ | _____ |
| _____ | _____ |
| _____ | _____ |

Signature _____

Date _____

*Starting Small Groups—and Keeping them Going.* Copyright © 1995 Augsburg Fortress. May be reproduced for local use.

# Preparing your first meeting

People are looking for three things in the first meeting:

1. They want to know what the purpose of this group is.

2. They want to feel welcome and not embarrassed.

3. They want to sense that they'd miss out if they didn't return.

## Environmental issues

Consider the following when planning for a meeting, knowing that surroundings and environment can make a big difference in the discussion and the engagement of the participants.

- seating
- lighting
- acoustics
- temperature
- facilitator's position
- sight obstacles

## Before the meeting

- Develop a list of those in your group as well as a list of potential participants. Work with the small group coordinator, if your church has one.

- Find a cofacilitator or arrange this with the small group coordinator. Talk with that person to decide which tasks or responsibilities he or she will take on.

- Send out personal invitations and/or make phone calls.

- Contact host and make sure the facilities for the meeting are ready. Provide all group participants with directions to the meeting location.

- Make necessary child care arrangements if needed. Notify those who would use it.

- Review the material to be used: prepare yourself.

- Be sure necessary items are planned for: name tags, covenant sample, pencils.

- Design an agenda for the meeting. Think about how prayer will be used, when, and by whom.

- Pray for God's guidance for those still making a decision about participating and for God's blessing on the meeting. Pray for each participant in your group by name. Maintain a spirit of enthusiasm and expectation. Trust God.

Training Handout 17

*Starting Small Groups—and Keeping them Going.* Copyright © 1995 Augsburg Fortress. May be reproduced for local use.

# Seating at small groups

How the group is seated has an effect on the interaction of the participants. Discuss with the host how the seating should be arranged to provide maximum participation. Much will depend on what you have to work with, but there are some general principles to be aware of as you arrange the seating.

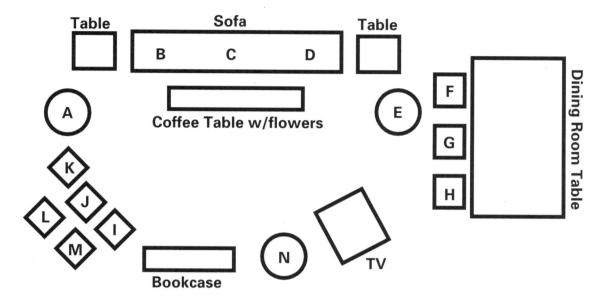

Study the living room design on this page and then respond to the questions. The places to sit are lettered A through N.

■ Where would you sit as the facilitator? Why?

■ Where would you suggest the cofacilitator sit?

■ If you were reluctant to participate, where would you sit?

■ Which persons would have poor eye contact with each other?

■ What would you say to a person who sat in the second row if there were other chairs empty?

■ How would you rearrange these chairs to enhance interaction and warmth?

■ What physical objects present a potential problem for interaction among members?

## Some things to remember:

■ The circle is the most helpful seating arrangement for small group sharing.

■ Motivation to speak is higher when you can see the faces of others.

■ Three people on a sofa means the center person always obstructs the eye contact of the persons on either end. Put pillows in the center so only two persons will occupy the sofa.

■ Certain seating arrangements encourage multiple conversations to develop.

■ People feel uncomfortable when the facilitator sits at a distance where eye contact is not easy.

■ Hearing becomes a problem when the seating is too far apart. Sometimes a participant who can't hear will be hesitant to make it known.

■ Two-tiered seating should always be avoided.

■ The host wants the room to look well planned, color coordinated, not crowded, and aesthetically attractive. The group facilitator wants the room to be conducive to small group interaction. They need to understand each other, communicate, and plan the seating arrangement together.

*Starting Small Groups—and Keeping them Going.* Copyright © 1995 Augsburg Fortress. May be reproduced for local use.

# Social events for small groups

Most small groups include a time to socialize over simple refreshments. This can be done as the participants arrive. Or it can be put at the end of the meeting so that those who need to leave at a certain time are free to do so without disrupting the session.

Invite participants to take turns bringing refreshments. Don't allow the refreshment time to become a competition in cooking or spending money on food. Remind the participants to keep it simple and easy. Keep in mind that some participants may have dietary restrictions.

As a way of getting started in an informal manner, some small groups start with a potluck meal (maybe including children). The evening can include a time of sharing and discussion of what members would like to see happen in their future meetings. Some have played games such as the LifeStories game (see Training Handout 13) as a way of getting better acquainted.

The down side of beginning with a meal is the amount of work involved. Some may shy away from that much of a commitment at first. Yet it remains an option to consider throughout the life of the group.

Plan special events for small groups that allow for socializing and enjoying each other in ways that the regular meeting doesn't allow for. People who are becoming well acquainted enjoy meeting other members of various families. At special events you can learn things about one another that may not be discovered in the regular meeting. Some things to consider are:

- Be sensitive to those who are single or without children or without relatives in the area.

- Use the holiday time to celebrate.

- The summer can be used for outdoor social events. Involve the group in thinking of options.

- Not everyone has extra money for social events or can afford a child care provider. Pool needs and resources.

- If you attend a movie or play or concert together try to include an opportunity to discuss it afterward.

- Plan well in advance so that calendars can be cleared. Use frequent reminders. Make assignments so that everyone is involved and responsible.

- Plan a social event with one or two other small groups which will facilitate a kind of sharing among groups.

- Plan a grand celebration of all the small groups. Make sure it fits into the church calendar and allows the participants to share their experiences, enjoy themselves, and gain enthusiasm for this aspect of ministry. Have each small group present a poster, a skit, a song, or something special that the others will enjoy.

- Plan an event that will involve visiting a place where one of the group's participants works, which might be of social interest.

- Plan an event that will combine a social experience with a service opportunity, like serving food at a feeding center or registering voters.

 *Starting Small Groups—and Keeping them Going.* Copyright © 1995 Augsburg Fortress. May be reproduced for local use.

# A: Ministry task ideas

■ Go together to serve at a soup kitchen or homeless shelter.

■ Collect food and clothing for a food shelf and clothes closet.

■ Identify a need not being met at your church and offer to be responsible for it for six months or so.

■ Offer to help paint the home, shovel the walk, or mow the lawn, of an elderly person, taking turns.

■ Have a letter-writing event where you all write a letter to an elected official about a common concern.

■ Visit a senior citizen home and take the time to sit with elderly people who have few, if any, visitors. Call ahead. Find out from staff what they might enjoy as part of the visit.

■ Make a video together that would address an important or needed service in your community.

■ Go together to visit an emergency waiting room in a large hospital. Sit and observe. Listen and feel. Come back and discuss.

■ Make an inspirational collage together around a theme from your group study and give it to someone.

■ Find out what someone in your group is doing as a volunteer and join in, or see what ideas come from what some are doing.

■ Find a task at your church that you haven't done before. Try it for a period. Switch male and female roles. Report back.

■ Be in contact with your pastor and other church leaders to learn what ministry tasks are needed in the church. Pick one and implement it.

# B: Welcoming the stranger

To welcome new members to the group, consider the following:

■ Encourage participants to invite friends. Tell them when it might be best to bring their friends. Some people feel more comfortable joining a group after a regular break in the group schedule, to avoid disturbing group dynamics.

■ See that the material and agenda for the meeting easy to follow.

■ Announce at the beginning that the group is open to people at various levels in their knowledge of the Bible or the Christian faith and people who are not members or your church.

■ Let people know that the small group is a place of exploration. It is a place where everyone is welcome and everyone's experience is valid.

■ Be sure that new people are welcomed and recognized. Introduce participants who are not already known to the group.

■ If comments are made that might make a new person feel awkward, break in and remind the group that not everyone may be of the same mind or understand what is being said. Or you might use the moment to get a second opinion by saying, "Jane, you come from a different background in the church. How do you see this question?"

■ Do not coerce new people to read aloud unless you know them well enough. On the other hand, don't assume that new people are biblically illiterate either. They may be far ahead of others in the group.

■ Do not let church membership be the hidden agenda. Remember that meaningful relationships are used by the Holy Spirit to bring about changes.

**Training Handout 20**

*Starting Small Groups—and Keeping them Going.* Copyright © 1995 Augsburg Fortress. May be reproduced for local use.

# A: Signs of a healthy small group

No two groups function exactly alike. There are some common elements that indicate health and growth. The following list is not exhaustive, but is intended as a guide to help you recognize important issues in group life.

- **Covenant or Contract:** A shared understanding of the group's purpose and the general expectations of each participant.

- **Commitments:** The disciplines and agreements which the group is willing to adopt in order to accomplish its agreed-upon purpose.

- **Presence:** As participants learn to be present to one another, they give themselves to others.

- **Caring:** The quality of life together in which participants learn how to love each other, support each other, and develop care for one another.

- **Content:** A central focus for study in order to know God and ourselves better.

- **Communication:** Relationships build through storytelling, active listening and the art of asking questions.

- **Feelings and vulnerability:** These are an important part of life together. People express feelings when trust is developed.

- **Action:** Love is an action word. As the participants experience love, they are motivated to become doers of the word, both individually and together.

- **Prayer:** Most participants don't really experience Christian community until they take time to pray together.

- **Jesus Christ:** The center of community and the one who transforms lives.

# B: Things that choke a small group

Small group facilitators will be able to read warning signs as they appear and deal with the problems before they begin to choke the life of a group. Some of them are:

- No clearly defined purpose
- Autocratic leadership
- Not focusing on purpose
- Inadequate physical setting
- Spiritual self-righteousness
- Confidences betrayed
- Not starting or quitting on time
- Talking about the sins of others
- Repeated absenteeism or lateness

- Too much talk by only a few
- Too much attention needed for one person's problem
- Material that does not get at feelings
- Unprepared facilitator
- One person's agenda dominating
- Denial of signs given to end the group
- Never enough time for the ministry component
- The group becoming too large
- No movement toward group prayer

*Starting Small Groups—and Keeping them Going.* Copyright © 1995 Augsburg Fortress. May be reproduced for local use.

# How to deal with monopolizers and onlookers

## Monopolizers

Groups normally have some participants who talk more than others. Occasionally these people monopolize the conversation and it becomes a problem. Others are not given a chance to talk, and become discouraged or silently irritated.

The following steps can be used to deal with these people:

1. On your first group meeting discourage anyone from dominating the group. Ask each participant to feel free to share, but be sensitive to the danger of monopolizing.

2. Don't be afraid to break in. Praise one of the monopolizer's statements and then raise a new question or ask for others to respond.

3. Do not sit directly across from these people. This limits eye contact and diffuses power. Monopolizers are encouraged by eye contact.

4. Don't respond to these participants' comments when they carry on too long. Response encourages more talk.

5. If the problem persists you can talk to the monopolizer alone after the meeting or over the phone. It may help to include yourself by saying "I've noticed that you and I do most of the talking. Let's see if we can encourage others by our talking less next time." Seek this person's help in getting wider participation by those who talk less.

6. Begin sharing around the circle and end with the person who tends to monopolize. Ask for responses from those who haven't spoken yet.

7. Express appreciation to the group for the willingness of everyone to share and the encouragement given by the group to see that everyone's participation is important.

8. After a few meetings, ask participants to write on an unsigned sheet of paper suggestions for improving group dynamics. Read these suggestions aloud to the group.

■ What other ways have you found helpful in handling the person who monopolizes?

## Onlookers

These people are not destructive to your group, but may need some encouragement to participate in the group discussion. People are different and some need more time or help in self-disclosure.

The following ideas may help:

1. Remember, it is alright for some participants to be silent. Their presence is a gift. The facilitator's role is to encourage, not to manipulate or coerce.

2. On some questions it is best to go around the circle giving responses. Vary this. Try not to start with the onlookers, but rather give them time to think of what to say.

3. Feel free to ask at an appropriate moment what these participants think or what their experience has been. Sometimes a direct question will help the onlookers feel affirmed and noticed.

4. When these people do speak, affirm the contribution. Thank them.

5. Divide the group into pairs or triads at times. Smaller groupings make discussion easier for some.

6. Be sensitive to the areas or things that onlookers feel at ease about. If they are knowledgeable or experienced in specific areas, find ways for them to talk about these. In a group task, some onlookers will take leadership and responsibility.

7. Spend a minute or two with these people before or after the meeting. Ask them how they feel about the group and if they feel comfortable participating. Let them know that their contribution is appreciated.

8. If participants feel loved and accepted for who they are, they are more likely to contribute.

■ What other ways have you found helpful in drawing the onlooker into the group discussion?

Training Handout 22

# A: Why groups terminate

All groups come to an end. Rarely is there one single cause. Here are ten common reasons for group termination.

1. **The group divides** to form two new groups. Often groups birth other groups in order to accommodate further growth. This is the ideal way for a group to end.

2. **The stated length of time expires.** Many groups disband because they began with a clearly defined time span for existence. However, a set time may not be the ideal reason to end a group. An agreement to continue might be needed.

3. **The goal is accomplished.** Rarely is the goal of relationship building completed. The ending of ministry groups, on the other hand, easily fits into this reason.

4. **The group explodes in conflict.** Unfortunately, small groups are not immune to the conflicts which can erupt in any church. If it happens, conflict usually occurs early in a group's life.

5. **A covenant has not been secured.** Lacking group norms or agreement on purpose, the attendance and behavior of the group participants disintegrates to the point where all agree that continuance is fruitless.

6. **A conscious decision is made to terminate,** for whatever reason. It may happen because of schedule conflicts, participants moving out of town, the desire to try something new, or a plan to reform the group. This is a logical choice on the part of the group participants.

7. **Group leadership is not sufficient** or not matched to the agenda of the group. Ministry groups and support and recovery groups are susceptible to leadership failure. Discipleship groups are as well, but because of their nature, they tend to be more forgiving of inadequate facilitators.

8. **Poor administration.** Lack of planning causes members to give up and not participate. Poor administration is normally a result of insufficient leadership.

9. **Conflict with other church programs.** Competition among activities is very common in most churches due to the limited time people have. Group participants are forced to choose between small group attendance or participation in something else. This situation reflects a philosophy of ministry that sees groups as just another programmatic option, rather than a centerpiece of the church's pastoral ministry.

10. **Members are not compatible.** This causes termination to be a logical choice, not necessarily fueled by conflict. For example, one group had members at both ends of the adult age span. They liked each other, but their interests and needs were too dissimilar. They decided to disband on amicable terms and then they all joined other groups.

# B: How to terminate a group gracefully

Remember that it takes time to build community, togetherness, and mutual support. There is usually a period of struggle for every group.

When signs become apparent that the group is struggling, talk it over with your pastor or coordinator. There may be some steps taken that could save the group. Another person's opinion can help. Or it may be best to terminate the group.

If it seems best to terminate, try to finish out the present series or task on which you are working. Let the group know that you will continue until a certain date and then discuss the future.

If no one is showing up, or only a few, it might be best to talk with individual participants about the situation and then inform the other participants that the group will take some time off. Be sure the members know what is happening. Sometimes certain personalities just don't click together. It doesn't mean failure.

Once you have set a date to end your current group, take time to celebrate the good that has happened. Suggest options to the members for their future involvement. Express thanks. End on a positive note.

Training Handout 23

*Starting Small Groups—and Keeping them Going.* Copyright © 1995 Augsburg Fortress. May be reproduced for local use.

# Tree of small group leadership

■ **Which of these children reflect how you feel about facilitating a small group?**

■ **Use your imagination.**

Adapted from material from Menlo Park Presbyterian Church, 950 Santa Cruz Ave., Menlo Park, Calif. 94025

*Starting Small Groups—and Keeping them Going.* Copyright © 1995 Augsburg Fortress. May be reproduced for local use.

Training Handout 24

# Practical tips for small groups

- Create a comfortable relaxed atmosphere.

- Start and end on time.

- Focus on relationships.

- Don't get too routine, yet be consistent.

- If you are not prepared don't fake it. (Just be prepared.)

- If at all possible, sing together.

- Be creative with session content, not a slave to it.

- Incorporate an attitude of outreach and ministry.

- Don't hesitate to seek help from your pastor or coordinator.

- Be clear on schedules, responsibilities, and location of each meeting.

- Be responsible for your own child care.

- Let the group be responsible for recruiting others.

- Everyone in the group is important and should be encouraged to share.

- Sharing feelings is as important as facts. This sharing has healing potential.

- Allow talk about one's own sins, not the sins of others.

- Respect everyone's right to pass (not speak on a given question).

- Don't lecture or give long readings.

- Avoid the idea of right and wrong answers or right and wrong feelings.

- Maintain a balance between fun and seriousness.

- Don't let minor issues occupy major time.

- Make it non-threatening.

- Major in life stories and faith stories.

- Learn to be comfortable with silence.

Training Handout 25

*Starting Small Groups—and Keeping them Going.* Copyright © 1995 Augsburg Fortress. May be reproduced for local use.

# Promises to claim

Bible verses can become a source of encouragement and strength as you carry on your important role as lay pastoral leaders. Reflecting on one verse before each meeting and claiming the promise can give confidence and awareness of divine presence. Here is a beginning list of helpful promises from God's Word.

- "If any of you is lacking in wisdom, ask God, who gives to all generously and ungrudgingly, and it will be given to you. But ask in faith, never doubting" (James 1:5-6a).

- "Trust in the LORD with all your heart, and do not rely on your own insight. In all your ways acknowledge him, and he will make straight your paths" (Proverbs 3:5-6).

- "Peace I leave with you; my peace I give you. I do not give to you as the world gives. Do not let your hearts be troubled, and do not let them be afraid" (John 14:27).

- "[God] gives power to the faint, and strengthens the powerless....Those who wait for the LORD shall renew their strength, they shall mount up with wings like eagles, they shall run and not be weary, they shall walk and not faint" (Isaiah 40:29, 31).

- "Call to me and I will answer you, and will tell you great and hidden things that you have not known" (Jeremiah 33:3).

- "But you will receive power when the Holy Spirit has come upon you; and you will be my witnesses in Jerusalem, in all Judea and Samaria, and to the ends of the earth" (Acts 1:8).

- "May the God of steadfastness and encouragement grant you to live in harmony with one another, in accordance with Christ Jesus, so that together you may with one voice glorify God the Father of our Lord Jesus Christ" (Romans 15:5-6).

- "Who knows? Perhaps you have come to royal dignity for just such a time as this" (Esther 4:14b).

- "My grace is sufficient for you, for power is made perfect in weakness" (2 Corinthians 12:9).

- "For now we see in a mirror, dimly, but then we will see face to face. Now I know only in part; then I will know fully, even as I have been fully known. And now faith, hope, and love abide, these three; and the greatest of these is love" (1 Corinthians 13:12-13).

- "Beloved, let us love one another, because love is from God; everyone who loves is born of God and knows God.... No one has ever seen God; if we love one another, God lives in us, and his love is perfected in us" (1 John 4:7, 12).

- "Blessed are the poor in spirit, for theirs is the kingdom of heaven. Blessed are those who mourn, for they will be comforted. Blessed are the meek, for they will inherit the earth. Blessed are those who hunger and thirst for righteousness, for they will be filled" (Matthew 5:3-6).

- "If you offer your food to the hungry and satisfy the needs of the afflicted, then your light shall rise in the darkness and your gloom be like the noonday. The LORD will guide you continually, and satisfy your needs in parched places, and make your bones strong; and you shall be like a watered garden, like a spring of water, whose waters never fail" (Isaiah 58:10-11).

- "Simon, Simon, listen! Satan has demanded to sift all of you like wheat, but I have prayed for you that your own faith may not fail; and you, when once you have turned back, strengthen your brothers" (Luke 22:31).

- "And remember, I am with you always, to the end of the age" (Matthew 28:20b).

Training Handout 26

# Case studies

The following case studies describe situations one might encounter in a support or recovery small group. Use the material in one of the following ways:

1. In groups of three or four, review the multiple choice responses. There is not necessarily one correct answer. Choose one or more or add your own, then share why you chose the answer(s) you did.

2. Role-play the situation, trying out the various responses suggested in the multiple choice list. Discuss what was effective and ineffective.

3. In groups of three or four, read the situation and discuss the possible responses in the multiple choice list. What response is natural to you? What seems most helpful to the other person?

## Situation 1

It is the middle of the third meeting of your group. A woman who had been unusually silent for the first half of this meeting, makes a brief attempt to fight back tears and then begins to cry. No one says anything about it. What do you do?

a. Continue as if nothing out of the ordinary were happening.

b. Express concern and reassurance.

c. Encourage her to talk about the events in her life which may be upsetting her.

d. Other

## Situation 2

Throughout the meetings one of the men had been insisting that he has no problems. In the middle of the fifth meeting, the group attacks him for "hiding behind a mask." At the present moment the whole interaction seems to be gaining intensity. He seems to becoming more defensive. What do you do?

a. Nothing.

b. Change the subject.

c. Say that he is not going to get anything out of the group if he does not put anything into it.

d. Ask him how he feels about what they are saying.

e. Remind the group that this is not a therapy group—not for confrontation but support.

f. Other

## Situation 3

A member of your group is constantly talking. When she doesn't have the entire group's attention, she starts a conversation with the person next to her. Her talking interferes with the main discussion. She continues for several minutes and gives no sign of stopping. What do you do?

a. Draw her into the main discussion by inviting her to tell the whole group what she is talking about.

b. Ask that there be only one conversation at a time.

c. Say that it sounds like a nursery school—everyone wants to talk, but no one wants to listen.

d. Say that there are two conversations going on.

e. Other

## Situation 4

In your fourth meeting, one of the men seems unusually quiet and despondent. Finally someone asks about his behavior and he replies that his wife just left him, and there is no reason to go on. He adds that in a heated argument he hit her, but that was no reason for her to leave. How would you respond?

a. Ask if you can talk about this further after the meeting.

b. Offer your concern and support for him in this tough situation.

c. Set aside the group's agenda to listen to the man's story.

d. Other

Training Handout 27

*Starting Small Groups—and Keeping them Going.* Copyright © 1995 Augsburg Fortress. May be reproduced for local use.

# Ongoing facilitator training topics

- ☐ Servant leadership
- ☐ Helping shy people
- ☐ Recruiting participants
- ☐ Role of the cofacilitator
- ☐ How to facilitate sharing
- ☐ Confession of sins
- ☐ Learning listening skills
- ☐ Use of Scripture
- ☐ Confrontation
- ☐ Male and female participation
- ☐ Referrals
- ☐ Special interest groups
- ☐ Worship and singing in small groups
- ☐ Groups that are not groups
- ☐ Encouraging group prayer
- ☐ Groups at the work place
- ☐ Discovering people's gifts
- ☐ Left brain, right brain, whole brain
- ☐ Group tasks and projects
- ☐ When to change groups
- ☐ Handling difficult people
- ☐ Challenging people

- ☐ Intimacy
- ☐ Keeping love at the center of small groups
- ☐ Follow up on missing participants; absenteeism
- ☐ Planning social events
- ☐ The empty chair concept
- ☐ Keeping small groups fun
- ☐ Avoiding cliques
- ☐ What to read about small groups
- ☐ Confidentiality
- ☐ Art of asking questions
- ☐ Shared leadership
- ☐ How to avoid burnout
- ☐ Choosing material
- ☐ Keeping Christ at the center
- ☐ Child care
- ☐ When the facilitator moves away
- ☐ Achieving genuine community
- ☐ When the pastor leaves
- ☐ Balancing relationships and content
- ☐ When to call an end to your group
- ☐ Helping newcomers fit in

*Starting Small Groups—and Keeping them Going.* Copyright © 1995 Augsburg Fortress. May be reproduced for local use.

**Training Handout 28**

# The need to listen

- Listening affirms people. Listening invites them to share their story and acknowledges their personhood.

- Being listened to is a basic spiritual need of every person. We can learn much about listening from the life of Jesus. In Mark 10:46-52 we read that even in the crowded streets of Jericho Jesus heard the cry of blind Bartimaeus. It says he called Bartimaeus to himself and listened to him. Perhaps for the first time this blind beggar felt listened to. Jesus had a way of drawing people out.

- Listening helps the speaker to sort out and clarify his or her thoughts and feelings. Thoughts get disentangled by talking about them to someone who is listening. When a person feels safe and unhurried, there is a greater willingness to express what's really going on.

- Effective listening encourages the speaker to continue talking. Very often the first problem mentioned is not the real one. As the speaker continues, the conversation moves toward root causes or the primary hurt. Being comfortable with pauses is important.

- Effective listening will not answer questions that aren't being asked. Proverbs 18:13 says, "If one gives answer before hearing, it is folly and shame."

- Effective listening is not uncomfortable with emotions being expressed. People can sense when their tears or their anger is unsettling to the listener.

- Sometimes a simple touch can say "I hear you." Squeezing someone's hand can let the person know you hear.

- Listening is not a passive activity. Listening means entering imaginatively into the other person's situation, fighting distractions, and concentrating.

- Listening means asking "What is this person saying to me? What does he or she really mean?" A teacher once asked her fourth grade class, "What is listening?" One girl answered, "Listening is wanting to hear."

- Listening puts greater emphasis on acceptance and understanding than on advice or answers. As a person experiences compassion and acceptance, they are freer to work out their problems or questions.

- Listening is a skill to be learned little by little. It takes time and patience.

- We listen through many layers or wrappings. It might be our own theology, politics, or background. A good listener cuts through these layers in order to hear what the speaker is really saying.

**Exercise:** Choose one of the above and share an experience where this was true for you.

Training Handout 29

*Starting Small Groups—and Keeping them Going.* Copyright © 1995 Augsburg Fortress. May be reproduced for local use.

# Listening through our own theological layers

**Exercise:** Pair up with another person, read this story and answer the questions.

A person in your small group begins to tell about their daughter who is living with a man, but not married. The speaker begins to unfold her feelings about this, her disagreement, her concern for her daughter's relationship with God, the need to repent. She wonders why her daughter doesn't have the same values she was brought up with and wonders where she failed as a parent.

Which of the following comments would be a likely response you would make, and why? How would you show by your listening that you care? Note the theological layer identified with each possible response. Does it fit?

1. "I know exactly how you feel. We have the same problem in our family. Youth today don't seem to have the same values we have, do they?"

**Theological layer:** There is only one right and wrong way to look at things. The way I was taught about right and wrong is the criteria by which I judge others. The world is really getting worse—there is not as much concern for right and wrong as there used to be.

2. "It sounds like you really care about your daughter and that you're wondering how to let her know that you love her."

**Theological layer:** Relationships are the most important thing; compassion is the bottom line—more important than dos or don'ts.

3. "I sometimes wonder if the church shouldn't be more direct in letting people know what the Bible says about right and wrong."

**Theological layer:** There is a place for the law as well as the gospel in our theology. The third use of the law is to teach us how to live and we ought to respect that use of the law. The gospel does not exclude directives on how to live.

4. "Don't feel bad. Young people face different pressures than we did when we were that age. I've come to be much more accepting of cohabitation before marriage in some situations."

**Theological layer:** One's theology is always undergoing change as we apply the biblical teachings to today's context. It's OK for one's theology to undergo development.

5. "Have you had a chance to talk to your daughter about how you feel? Are you able to listen to each other?"

**Theological layer:** Compassion includes listening. It is critical to listen to people in order to know how to be compassionate.

6. "We've made it clear to our children that when they visit us with their opposite sex friends they will sleep in separate bedrooms until they are married. They know how we feel."

**Theological layer:** It's OK to stand up for one's convictions without insisting that others agree with us. Being clear on what you believe and ask for is critical in relationships.

7. "It sounds like you are blaming yourself for a choice your daughter has made."

**Theological layer:** People have to be free to make their own decisions and live the results. We do not have to save the world. That's God's job.

8. Other

Training Handout 30

*Starting Small Groups—and Keeping them Going.* Copyright © 1995 Augsburg Fortress. May be reproduced for local use.

# References

Baranowski, Arthur B. *Creating Small Faith Communities: A Plan for Restructuring the Parish and Renewing Catholic Life.* Cincinnati: St. Anthony Messenger Press, 1988.

Barna, George. *What Americans Believe: An Annual Survey of Values and Religious Views in the United States.* Ventura, Calif.: Regal Books, 1991.

Bonhoeffer, Dietrich. *Life Together: A Discussion of Christian Fellowship.* New York: Harper and Row, 1954.

Callahan, Kennon L. *Twelve Keys to an Effective Church.* San Francisco: Harper San Francisco, 1983.

"Tree of Small Group Leadership" drawing on page 129 adapted from material from Menlo Park Presbyterian Church, 950 Santa Cruz Ave., Menlo Park, Ca. 94025.

George, Carl. *Prepare Your Church for the Future.* Tarrytown, New York: Fleming H. Revell Company, 1991.

Gorman, Julie A. *Community That Is Christian: A Handbook on Small Groups.* Wheaton, Ill.: Victor Books, 1993.

Hestenes, Roberta. "Building Christian Community through Small Groups."
Department of Christian Formation and Discipleship, Fuller Theological Seminary, Pasadena, Calif., 1985. Photocopy.

Hestenes, Roberta.
*Turning Committees into Communities.* Colorado Springs: Navpress, 1991.

Hestenes, Roberta. *Using the Bible in Small Groups.* Louisville, Ky.: Westminster Press, 1983.

Icenogle, Gareth Weldon. *Biblical Foundations for Small Group Ministry: an Integrational Approach.* Downers Grove, Ill.: InterVarsity Press, 1994.

Johnson, George S. *Following Jesus.* Minneapolis: Augsburg Fortress, 1995.

Johnson, Vivian Elaine. "The Art of Storytelling." Unpublished article.

Jones, E. Stanley. *The Reconstruction of the Church—On What Pattern.* Nashville: Abingdon,

Lewis, Sinclair. *Dodsworth.* New York: Random House, 1947.

*LifeStories: The Christian Version.* Created by Wilfred Bockelman, Truman Howell, and Vivian Johnson. Pomona, Calif.: Talicore, 1994.

McBride, Neal F. *How to Lead Small Groups.* Colorado Springs: NavPress, 1990.

Meyer, Richard C. *One Anothering: Biblical Building Blocks for Small Groups.* San Diego, Calif.: LuraMedia, 1990.

Miller, Keith. *Taste of New Wine.* Dallas: Word Books, 1965.

*Occasional Services: A Companion to Lutheran Book of Worship.* Minneapolis: Augsburg Fortress, 1982.

O'Connor, Elizabeth. *Call to Commitment.* New York: Harper & Row, 1963.

Rothauge, Arlin J. *Sizing Up a Congregation for New Member Ministry.* New York: The Episcopal Church Center, 1994.

Sample, Tex. *U.S. Lifestyles and Mainline Churches.* Louisville, Ky.: Westminster/ John Knox Press, 1990.

Schaller, Lyle E. *Strategies for Change.* Nashville, Tenn.: Abingdon Press, 1993.

Schaller, Lyle E. *Assimilating New Members.* Creative Leadership Series. Nashville, Tenn.: Abingdon Press, 1978.

Towns, Elmer L. *10 of Today's Most Innovative Churches.* Ventura, Calif.: Regal Books, 1990.

"Unite and Conquer." *Newsweek,* February 5, 1990, pages 50-54.

Wuthnow, Robert. *Sharing the Journey: Support Groups and America's New Quest for Community.* New York: Free Press/Macmillan, 1994.

# Resources

## Foundational

*10 Of Today's Most Innovative Churches,* by Elmer L. Towns. Ventura, Calif.: Regal Books, 1990. This book describes what these ten churches are doing, how they are doing it, and how others can apply their ideas in their church setting.

*20/20 Vision,* by Dale E. Galloway. Portland, Ore.: Scott Publishing Company, 1990. Source of inspiration, motivation, and ideas for building a small group ministry.

*Beyond Church Growth,* by Robert E. Logan. Tarrytown, N.Y.: Fleming H. Revell Company, 1989. A comprehensive, foundational resource for helping a church to grow by more than numbers.

*Bringing Your Church Back to Life,* by Daniel Buttry. Valley Forge, Pa.: Judson Press, 1989. A description of survival mentality in churches in a series of Bible studies and small group processes for reviewing the church's life and ministry.

*Building Bridges: The Art and Practice of Evangelistic Calling.* Grand Rapids, Mich.: Church Development Resources, 1988. A basic how-to book connecting friendship evangelism, front-door evangelism, and small group evangelism with visitation evangelism.

*The Business of Paradigms: Discovering the Future Series,* by Joel Arthur Barker. 1990. Videotape (38 minutes) that helps leaders understand the natural resistance to change and the effects of that resistance.

*Life Together: A Discussion of Christian Fellowship,* by Dietrich Bonhoeffer. New York: Harper and Row, 1954. A penetrating and profound treatment of the essentials of Christian community.

*The Once and Future Church: Reinventing the Congregation for a New Mission Frontier,* by Loren B. Mead. Bethesda, Md.: The Alban Institute, Inc., 1991. Covers development of mission fields and the state of change in which churches find themselves today.

*The Power of Vision: Discovering the Future Series,* by Joel Arthur Barker. 1990. Videotape (30 minutes) resource for understanding the importance of vision.

*Seven Steps and You Will Grow,* by Neal R. Boese. Erlanger, Ky.: Seven Steps Ministries, 1991. Outlines a process for church renewal and growth that emphasizes adult education, spiritual gifts, and God's call to mission.

*Sharing The Journey: Support Groups and America's New Quest for Community,* by Robert Wuthnow. New York: Free Press/Macmillan, 1994. Analyzes the small group movement and the impact it is having on society and the church.

*What Americans Believe: An Annual Survey of Values and Religious Views in the United States,* by George Barna. Ventura, Calif.: Regal Books, 1991. An annual survey of values and religious views in the United States.

*Where Do We Go From Here?* by Ralph W. Neighbour Jr. Houston, Texas: Touch Publications, Inc., 1990. Provides guidance for making the transition from a program-based church to a ministry built on cells.

## Small Groups

Intersections Small Group Series. Minneapolis: Augsburg Fortress, 1995. In addition to *Starting Small Groups—and Keeping Them Going,* the series presently includes twelve study guides for discipleship groups and support and recovery groups. See back cover for ordering information.

*The Bible and Life: God's Message for Today,* by Joy P. Clarke. Explores the basic message of the Bible and how it serves as a means of divine grace for life.

*Captive and Free: Insights from Galatians,* by Walter F. Taylor Jr. A Bible study of Galatians that addresses God's gift of freedom from destructive patterns to a liberating freedom for trust, hope, and love.

*Caring and Community: Perspectives from Ephesians,* by Robert H. Albers. This study focuses on the important life support we gain through Christian fellowship in an age of personal isolation.

*Death and Grief: Healing through Group Support,* by Harold Ivan Smith. Helps those who grieve to bring their stories, anger, and bewilderment to a small group.

*Divorce: Survival and Hope,* by Russell E. Fink and Barbara Owen-Fink. Guides divorced and separated people in dealing with the transition from being married to being single.

*Faith: Confidence and Doubt in Daily Life,* by Martin E. Marty. A Bible study that helps small groups explore personal faith in life-cycle experiences-moods and situations, joy and discouragement, confidence and doubt.

*\*Following Jesus: Encouragement from the Beatitudes for a Troubled World,* by George S. Johnson. Helps participants move beyond a world dominated by greed, violence, and domination to one of compassion, harmony, and community.

*Jesus: Divine and Human,* by John L. Heagle. Explores what a difference it can make to have Jesus as Savior, teacher, healer, reconciler, and friend.

*Men and Women: Building Communication,* by Tina and Dennis Korte. Examines male-female relationships, differences, and commonalities and helps develop skills to improve communication between men and women.

*A starter resource for discipleship groups.

*Peace: Christian Living in a Violent World*, by Mary I. Farr. A Bible study that explores the peace of God, and what wholeness and health, contentment and security and mean for one's life.

*Praying: Meeting God in Daily Life*, by Lyn Klug. A Bible study that examines the depth and power of prayer, the personal nature and lifestyle of prayer, and a variety of prayer forms and occasions.

*Self-Esteem: Encouraging Self and Others*, by Eddie Jane Pelkey and Irene Getz. Participants explore the sometimes-difficult balance between loving self and acting responsibly toward others.

*Beginning a Ministry Team Group*, by Kent Odor. Littleton, Colo.: Serendipity, 1991. Activities and studies for building team spirit and community.

*Biblical Foundations for Small Group Ministry: An Integrational Approach*, by Gareth Weldon Icenogle. Downers Grove, Ill.: InterVarsity Press, 1994. Explores the why of small group ministry more than the how.

*Faith Sharing for Small Church Communities: Questions and Commentaries on The Sunday Readings*, edited by Arthur Branowski. Cincinnati: St. Anthony Messenger Press, 1993. Questions based on lectionary cycles A, B, and C that explore the Bible texts and help make application to daily life. Written for use by small groups.

*Community That Is Christian: A Handbook on Small Groups*, by Julie A. Gorman. Wheaton, Ill.: Victor Books, 1993. This book lays out the quest for community with clear analysis and the latest insights from the social sciences.

*Creating Small Faith Communities: A Plan for Restructuring the Parish and Renewing Catholic Life*, by Arthur B. Baranowski. Cincinnati: St. Anthony Messenger Press, 1988. A review of how the Roman Catholic church is experiencing spiritual renewal through small groups.

*LifeStories: The Christian Version*, created by Wilfred Bockelman, Truman Howell, and Vivian Johnson. Pomona, Calif.: Talicore, 1994. Available at Augsburg Fortress outlets, or by calling Talicore at 1-800-433-GAME. A board game that helps people share their stories and enjoy conversation. Includes faith story questions.

*Rapha's Handbook for Group Leaders*, by Richard Price, Pat Springle, and Joe Kloba. Houston, Texas: Rapha Publishing, 1991. Resource on group dynamics covering the group environment and mechanics, family systems, the healing process, and much more.

*Small Group Ministry With Youth*, by David R. Veerman: SP Publications, Inc., 1992. Explains why youth need small group ministry and gives examples of effective small group ministry with youth.

*Transforming Bible Study*, by Walter Wink. Nashville, Tenn.: Abingdon Press, 1989. A revised edition of his earlier book on Bible study. Innovative in combining biblical information with readers' experience leading to personal transformation.

*Turning Committees into Communities*, by Roberta Hestenes. Colorado Springs, Colo.: Navpress, 1991. This 32-page book provides basic helps to guide committees from burnout to caring, Christian communities.

*Using the Bible In Groups*, by Roberta Hestenes. Louisville, Ky.: Westminster Press, 1983. A practical book on the use of the Bible in small groups plus tips on building relationships.

*You Can Grow in a Small Group*, by Ronald J. Lavin. Lima, Ohio: C.S.S. Publishing Company, Inc., 1976. A detailed guide for developing *koinonia* groups in your church. The author has been developing small groups for more than 30 years.

## Evangelism

*Preparing Lay Callers for Community Outreach*, by Gary Wollersheim. Minneapolis: Augsburg Fortress, 1995. Complete resource for training church members to make calls on community residents. Part of a three part series for caller training.

*Preparing Lay Callers for Congregation Care*, by Diana Sickles. Minneapolis: Augsburg Fortress, 1995. Provides a process for training members to call on other members to extend pastoral care.

*Preparing Lay Callers for Visitor Follow-up*, by David F. Keener. Minneapolis: Augsburg Fortress, 1995. Provides complete training for church members to call on church visitors.

*Reaching the Unchurched: Creating the Vision, Planning to Grow*, by Walt Kallestad and Tim Wright. Minneapolis: Augsburg Fortress, 1995. A 60-minute video workshop and accompanying workbook guides a planning committee through the process of developing a long-term plan for reaching unchurched people in the community.

*Sharing Your Faith with Friends, Relatives, and Neighbors*, by Paul Sorensen. Minneapolis: Augsburg Fortress, 1995. A six-session course designed for small group use. Provides Bible texts to study and practical help for participants to gain confidence in talking about their Christian faith with others. Includes a participant resource and leader guide.

*Worship and Outreach: New Services for New People*, by Donald M. Brandt. Minneapolis: Augsburg Fortress, 1994. A complete guide for churches that want to reach unchurched people by offering a new worship service.

## New Member Integration

*Assimilating New Members* Creative Leadership Series, by Lyle E. Schaller. Nashville, Tenn.: Abingdon Press, 1978. Overview of the process and challanges encountered in assimilating new members into a church.

*Discovering Spiritual Gifts: Spiritual Gifts Discovery in Small Groups,* by Paul R. Ford. Pasadena, Calif.: Charles E. Fuller Institute of Evangelism and Church Growth, 1991. Twelve-week course on spiritual gifts and gifts identification. Includes three tapes, leader materials, and spiritual gifts inventory.

*Make New Members Active Members: Strategies for Incorporating New Members,* by Patricia A. Haller. Minneapolis: Augsburg Fortress, 1995. A step-by-step guide for moving regular visitors into active membership. Designed for the small to mid-sized church. Includes assessment tools, spiritual gifts inventory, and other practical helps.

*Membership Class,* by Dan Reiland, El Cajon, Calif.: Injoy, 1991. Step-by-step course for new members combined with spiritual gifts discernment and ministry connection. A basic course that can be easily adapted and customized. Includes outlines, gifts inventory and audio tapes. Student materials may be copied from leader's manual.

*Sizing Up a Congregation for New Member Ministry,* by Arlin J. Rothauge. New York: The Episcopal Church Center, 1994. Describes the operational styles of churches by size.

*Trenton Spiritual Gifts Analysis,* Pasadena, Calif.: Fuller Evangelistic Association, 1983. This instrument is helpful for new members as they begin to identify and utilize their spiritual gifts within the body of Christ. One version is designed for liturgical churches. Others are available.

*Unfinished Evangelism: More Than Getting Them in the Door,* by Tim Wright. Minneapolis: Augsburg Fortress, 1995. Explores new approaches and offers practical strategies for for transforming a faith community into active, mission-focused members.

*Your Spiritual Gifts—Can Help Your Church Grow,* by Peter C. Wagner. Ventura, Calif.: Regal Books, 1979. Foundational resource for understanding and communicating the importance of spiritual gifts.

## Periodicals

*Buena Vista Ink,* Roman Catholic newsletter on small group. Write to Box 5474, Arvada, CO 80006-5474.

*The Evangelizing Congregation,* published by the Division for Congregational Ministries, Evangelical Lutheran Church in America. Contact the ELCA Distribution Service at 800-328-4648 to order.

*Net Results,* published by the National Evangelistic Association of the Christian Church (Disciples of Christ.) Call 806-762-8094 for subscription information.

*Perspectives: The Changing Church,* produced by Prince of Peace Publishing Inc., Burnsville, Minnesota. Call 800-874-2044 to be put on their mailing list.

*Practically Speaking: The Audiomagazine for Today's Church Leaders,* published by Augsburg Fortress, Minneapolis, Minnesota. Nine one-hour tapes available by subscription. Includes interviews, columns, and discussions on a wide range of subjects such as contemporary worship, evangelism, leadership, and spirituality. Call 800-328-4648.

*Voices,* newsletter of the house church movement. Write to Christian Smith, 3125 Stanford Drive, Durham, NC 27707.